Wisdom & Dust

Poems by

Neil McCrea

NeoPoiesis Press, LLC

NeoPoiesis Press
P.O. Box 38037
Houston, TX 77238-8037

www.neopoiesispress.com

Neil McCrea – Wisdom & Dust
ISBN 978-0-981-99847-3 (paperback : alk. paper)
    1. Poetry. I.   McCrea, Neil

Printed in the United States of America.

First Edition

Acknowledgements

Cover image "Old Man in Boat" by Natalie Sharar

Maps has previously appeared in the April 2009 issue of ETC: a
Review of General Semantics   (Volume Sixty-Six, number Two)

Henry has previously appeared in Knock #11

Cosmopolitan and Learning to Dodge Bullets have previously
appeared in Candy (NeoPoiesis Press, LLC)

*This book is dedicated to
Jo Fleming Waspersoon
for lending me her car
after vandals had blown mine
to kingdom come,
and to Christine Robart
who is the inspiration
for any bits of joy
to be found in this tome,
without whom it would be naught
but a litany of woe.*

Contents

Wisdom and Dust

Bare knees on cold linoleum
five year old in fervent first prayer
hands clasped, eyes raised
watching the sun glint
from dancing dust motes
and mistaking them for angels.

Sunday school sermon on Solomon
an energetic ingénue of a teacher
said God promised Solomon any one thing
and when Solomon asked for wisdom
he received it
and through wisdom
was granted wealth, power and the love of many women.
No fool, our five year old
began to pray for wisdom daily.

Any prayer is always answered
and as the child entered adulthood
no one dared doubt his intellect
An academic firebrand,
ivory towers tremble at the weight of his written word.
But the outside world wearies of wisdom
three divorces have left him in debt.
His children idolize pop stars
while he blows dust from his books
watching the motes plummet earthward.

Joyeux Noel

The slow susurration of snow falling
meant Christmas to the boy
even though the holiday was weeks past.
Awkwardly trundling
to meet neighbor girl, Noel.
He was happy in the new knowledge
that her name meant Christmas, too.

A silent and sad-eyed six,
he seemed older.
The boy was brainy
and built box-like.
Sorely lacking socialization
his sole playful peer,
the strawberry haired
darling daughter
of the haughty yuppies
next door.

Playmate plans were made
over morning cocoa.
Neophyte naughtiness
to occur in the neighbor's
frost filled garden.
"Show me and I'll show you."

The snow pants are a struggle,
and when the drawers are dropped
he pauses, puzzled,
staring at his penis.
"It's hard!?" the girl giggles.
Still in silent appreciation
he says nothing.

2

"Can I touch it?"
He gives a nearly negligible nod
and slowly smiles
as her cautious hand
wraps him in human warmth.

It must have been mere moments,
but their time stretched to the eternal.
Children of Adam and Eve
tasting the forbidden in a frosty garden.
So was her father God or the serpent?
Did his actions punish the fallen,
or give rise to the knowledge of good and evil?

There may have been yelling
but it was the conjunction
of boot to boy
that interrupted them.
Soaring over the snow
the boy felt paradise lost
as he was punted by paternal forces.
"Perverted child", a parting word
as he pulled up his pants
and wandered home.

Clutching his guts,
he sold mom
on a tummy ache,
and spent the day in his room.
A mailbox bundle
of candy canes
arrived that evening
accompanied by
a crayon scrawled
note from Noel.

The boy's parents are perplexed
when the room bound boy
curses the candy,
heaps hate upon the girl
and quietly cries
that Christmas is unfair.

Ars Poetica in Infancy

Rhythm contracts written
'twixt car and crayon.

Near silent seat bounce
on Sunday Symphony matinee

Improvised grass dance
in Spring packed playground

Cardamom creations for a clean palette
goose Granny's cooking

The arts in childhood remembered
give ease to adulthood's angst.

Henry

He agreed with the therapist. Trying to recover repressed memories through hypnosis is too prone to suggestion. Standard psychoanalysis, dream interpretation and time would hopefully do the trick. The lost and fragmented memories were muddied tracks on kitchen linoleum. The intruder who left the tracks certainly visited the refrigerator, but it was impossible to interpret the route.

A lonely boy throughout junior high, his parents bought him a hamster and an elaborate jungle of plastic tubing. He named the tan and white fur ball Henry. He wanted Henry clean. The cage would be cleared of rodent shit every night at 8pm. He knew Henry had more shit in him, and he wanted it gone. A slow squeezing of the little abdomen never failed to produce results. The critter grew bug-eyed, and opened his jaws wide in silent pain every evening as tiny pellets were forced from its ass. Of course, this could not go on forever and eventually Henry was squeezed too tight. All future hamsters would be named Henry as well, none of them lasted as long.

The rocking horse was smooth and solid. It had minimal decor, but was comfortable and soothing to look at and ride upon. A carpenter friend of his father's had built it for his little sister. When no one was around he would hug it and weep. Heavy sobs came with every stroke of the seat. One evening he snuck out of the house with it. He dropped it off a freeway overpass, causing a seven car pileup. When one car caught fire, the ecstatic sense of freedom he felt almost caused him to linger too long.

"Son, I'd like you to meet Henry. He is your father's first friend in this new town and he's been very good to us. Now, he sounds funny because he is deaf and he's never heard what words sound like. You must remember to always look him straight in the eye

6

when you speak to him, because otherwise he won't be able to understand you. He's going to take care of you while your father and I are away. If you're good, maybe you can watch as he makes you a toy in his wood shop. ---- Henry, you said you weren't going to drink around my son. I can smell it on your breath from here. Just rein it in until we get back."

He blew off a quarter of college. Living off of student aid, he haunted the local dive bars and seduced middle-aged women. Finding sex partners had never been as easy as this. He did his best to bathe in tits, ass, and pussy. A sizable pride in his intellectual abilities drove him back to school. An odd moment of common sense led him to take advantage of the school clinic's free battery of STD screenings. When a nurse inserted a complicated looking swab up his urethra, something broke deep inside his mind.

As a small child he was in awe of the doctor's office and examining room. They were the cleanest rooms he had ever seen. His eyes grew large as he noticed the large collection of lollipops in a jar on the doctor's desk. The adults talked for an endless time, but he eventually was given a darkly purple, grape lollipop. A short time later, he almost swallowed it whole as he watched disbelieving as the doctor inserted a complicated looking swab into his penis.

He once asked his parents about this unusual doctor's visit, but all he got was shrugs and a vague recollection that he suffered from urinary tract infections as a child. He never asked about it again, but to this day he continues to try and follow muddy footprints around his kitchen floor.

Man of God

I drank battery acid coffee
and hauled furniture at midnight.
My twelve year old sensibility
had little understanding
of transpiring events.

Foreigners milled about
speaking what amounted to moon man.
A blonde-crowned pate rose above,
our pastor, a Viking tainted Scotsman,
directed both movers and refugees
into the apartment in his basement.

My parents spoke of asylum denied to
refugees from a Reagan appointed dictator.
Some were Catholic, most Communist
but our Presbyterian pastor
saw only wronged souls
and gave them Sanctuary
from the feds.

Reflected in the Past's mirror
I see sights I ignored before.
North African victim of female circumcision
given medical aid and freedom
through his auspices.
An Iranian defectee
given shelter until he could find
a local mosque to favor.
Medical missions to Haiti
and famine relief to Ethiopia.

I'm often at odds with religion,
yet I find atheists who make my heart ache.
They glory in freedom from fables and fear,
revel in rebellion from rules
and recoil from responsibility to others.

8

My metaphysical meanderings
take me many miles from the orthodox
but I shall never scorn
the man of God
whose faith is an active one
whose mouth can't invoke the infernal
and whose every deed is filled
with risky altruism.

Prostitution

I disliked bull sessions,
those craven conventions
of brash bravado and mass machismo,
but a sophomore among seniors
appreciates acceptance
wherever he can find it.

The talk was ever of evaluation,
a grading of breasts and buttocks.
I denied a universal standard of beauty,
the girls I dug seldom scored high
in the endless ranking
of the bored boys behind
the metal shop.

This denial of their deeply held truths
led to their assumption of my inexperience.
Not one to lie, I let my virginity label me.
The boys made a burden of it,
a heavy weight holding me hostage,
coloring my comments,
and keeping me uncool.

Big Bill Bishop, b-baller and bad-ass
sought to save me.
His coach paid me periodically
to write reports and take tests
in Big Bill's name.
The school's star was swamped
with female fans.
Bill bartered with a few girls
who would be grateful for better grades.

Fallon was the first,
the Faulkner report fared favorably,
she promised I'd be pleased with the payment.
She swung like Salome
and sat me down sultan-like.
Inside the Impala,
lips locked and licked my length.
shiver and shake, jerk and squirt,
the course was quick but not quiet.
She sat up shocked,
"Still hard, Hon?
I guess we've got work to do."

After accepting the brief biography of Harper Lee,
Shonda showed up behind the bleachers.
Elegantly Ethiopian and deeply dark,
the bashful beauty seemed sad.
A brief nod and she kneeled.
Did I witness weeping?
"Wait! I don't want it like this!"
I lifted her and let her go.
She shook and shivered as she ran.
The papers flew and fluttered,
I shrugged and sighed,
"She could have kept them."

Heidi was a hesher,
and awed over her "A",
we made out to Maiden,
sucked to Sabbath,
and fucked fiery and fierce.
Sore, supine and sated
she confessed coyly,
"You could be my boyfriend,
if you knocked off the nerdiness."

After a legion of lunches
I went back to the bull sessions.
Puffed up with pride,
content that my virgin visage
had been replaced
by an aura of erotic experience.
They deftly deflated my ego,
with the words "whores don't count!"
How I hated them! How dare they
degrade my newfound darlings.
I harbored no illusions of intimacy,
I knew that I was but a tool
for the girls' academic advancement.
The only whore that I saw
was me.

Their Entire World

The universe didn't crack open,
though some part of them
thought it might.
They arose from the damp bedroll
and gazed at the Alabama morning dew
glistening on his motorcycle.
A new world's Adam and Eve,
struggling to cover their naked flesh,
their eyes lit with understanding,
even as they forgave each other
for having no one else to love.

Fast food parents worse than wage slaves,
gave him up before they grew grimmer.
State raised and never adopted,
he easily graduated
from state home
to juvenile detention.
To this day chocolate makes him gag,
the big bull of his wing
would melt the bars
to lube up the new kids
for his pleasure.
Two weeks in the world,
until a moment of manslaughter
sent him to the post grad world
of the state penn.

The Seventh sibling
she seemed to be surplus
it was as if no one could remember
how or why she had been born.

At ten, she got some attention,
her whiskey soaked straw father
would beat her whenever she spoke
to the neighborhood children.
Constantly frightened and miserable,
her battered soul recognized
the fear in her father,
not that she would be a slut
but that He desired
to use her as one.

A week before parole he got her letter,
at sixteen she discovered a sibling
she had never met.
Not needing to meet his parents
they rendezvoused at a Royal Fork.
He sat in silence
newly cognizant
that he had spoken to women
only a handful of times
in his whole life.
But the silence was warm with compassion,
and filled with an understanding
only they could share.
At length she uttered,
"Take me away from here."

On the road
odd jobs and petty crime
they felt close
and safe
and when the world failed to end
they felt normal.

Two years down the road,
new names in a new state,
steady jobs, a solid home
and a child on the way.
Surprisingly, their folks found them,
cops came and cuffed them,
the media went mad for a moment,
and they were made to notice
the world's wrath.

Sad and sympathetic,
the judge would have let them go
but for the thought
of the child they created.
Now they sit separated in stir,
reflecting on the only two years
when they felt happy.

A Threat of Rape

"I'm going to bend you over that wall
and fuck you up the ass!"
I figure he must be confused
didn't this fight start over the girls?

High school field trip
out after curfew
throwing Frisbees in the park
in the dark

volcanic bile threatens to rise
as he punches me twice in the gut
I can't breathe well enough to cough
as his buddy swings me around

asked along more for protection, than play
three drama club girls and a 90lb gay lad
thought my knuckle-dragging self
might come in handy

I stare at the sweatshirt
of a human sparkplug
SOU wrestling team in grey
the man behind me kicks my legs apart

after Frisbee, I recline on soft grass
and watch the girls swing
long limbed and coltish Ramona,
athletic Nikki, and delicate Kris
flighty David roams elsewhere

The kick hits metal
my knee brace a souvenir
from my last altercation
I'm not completely unacquainted with violence
I struggle

Did I nap?
China doll Kris is smoking with apes
the atmosphere reads tense
no nonsense in Nikki,
"We need to go now!"

The brace keeps me from falling
my shoulder threatens to dislocate
as I twist out of the arm lock
I swear I won't be the only one
who gets hurt in this fight

"We're not done with you yet!"
Drama girls must secretly run varsity cross-country
They sprint past me with thugs in tow
I'm too gimpy to run
body checking the brutes better serves the situation

"I've brought the police!,"
little David squeaks loudly
Bullies bolt from nothing I can see
I simmer & seethe
convinced I would have killed them

At the hostel I swagger sultan-like
boasting of bravery to beauties
while little David, openly gay at 16
quietly retires to his room

City Kids Hit County Fair for Kitschy Kicks

Apple munch crackerjack
first stop food forest
dozens of dough variants
fried fried fried
not sick but
giddy with grease
it's time to
go go go

Animal mimicry
not funny
but maybe mandatory
when perusing
the prize pigs.
"That pig's BIG"

"Win one for your woman!"
Bad at the b-ball bounce
the ring toss is rigged
hammer pounding bell ringing
nets a Guns N Roses do-rag
now worn sans irony
over one femme's
riot grrrl gear.

Teens time the rattletrap ride
with rubber monsters
planning brief blow jobs
in the dark
but burst unbuckled
and barely blown
into kinder filled daylight

18

and lightly leave
laughing down the midway.

Clip clop chain drop
a classic coaster
copped from an old
big city boardwalk
leaves all
in wind burnt wonder
and feeling frisky.

Big lights up
as the sun goes down
pallid pop stars
or jingoistic country crooners
hit the center stage
our kids
heckle hard
fondle freely
and
pass pass puff
until its time to go.

driving back
with snarky sarcasm
for the small town
unaware
the feelings are
reciprocated.

Honey on Boot Hill

Built in the branches of the spreading oak,
the hive drips golden upon the crumbling marble
of a long neglected headstone.

The man buried beneath
thought gunpowder
to be the scent of responsibility,
authorities with conflicting interests
conspired to make him a killer,
but he kept on killing
long after such duties had been asked of him,
so history made him infamous.

Illiterate and unimaginative,
the knowledge of his name living on
in pulps, paperbacks, flicks, television
and occasionally high cinema
would amaze and confound him.

Fickle fate spared his resting place
from the tawdry dealings of tourism,
and the name on the stone,
though true,
was not the name of the legend.

A dainty darling,
no doubt drawn by the scent
of sticky sweetness,
first spied the stone
when searching for a spot
for her paramour to paw at her.
The boy grew boorish and the girl bashful
in equal measure,

and the dead bore witness
to the end of the dalliance.

Surprising the spirits,
and herself,
the girl regularly returns to the site
in dappled daylight.

Thin lips clutch a clove cigarette
while pale hands trace the name
upon the stone.

There is a power to names.
A power to This name,
although it's history
is unknown to her and hers.

The urge building for weeks,
she finally declares her love
for the name on the stone,
and somewhere
the living and the dead
clasp hands . . .

. . . and dance.

Writer's Hands

A rolling stride from the theatre entrance
and I am upon the campus square
garbed Elizabethan,
the character of Mercutio
has yet to leave me.
Seeking revelry,
I spy her among lesser men.

Coltish Ramona, grown goddess like
High school fantasy now found
in a domain I dominate.
I shout her name
and bow with a rapier-scraping flourish.
The enamel of her teeth
must be coated with phosphorous
to light the evening so.

Such a sweet embrace she gives me,
I must swallow a stutter.
"I haven't seen you since high school.
How've you been?," she asks.
"Grand and glorious," I reply
as I take her hand to kiss.

"Your hands are so soft,
it's like you've never done a day of work in your life!"

I blanch at her words.
A hippy hyena says, "daaaamn"
and laughs long and hard.
The entire hacky sack set
mocks and mumbles.
I disengage and droop.

She blushes and apologizes,
"They're a writer's hands.
A writer's hands."

"It was good to see you again,"
I splutter and retreat.
Laughter from below
a Peruvian shepherd's hat
follows me.
A field away I halt.
Stopped by
Le Esprit de Escalier.

I should've responded.
Shown my sunken knuckles
to the hyena
and offered to demonstrate
how they got that way.
Or, salaciously suggested
that vaginal fluids
soften calluses quickly.

Too late for repartee
I fume and seek a party
to fight or fuck,
but end up drinking
and drinking
while rubbing my hands
as if I were a silent era
cinema villain.

Cosmopolitan

Earth goddess in youth
breasts of Paleolithic fantasy,
flat stomach and wide hips.
Sex with her was languorous and warm,
blanket wrapped and adrift
on a warm watered ocean,
but there were waves.

We met on set.
A student film, solidly sci-fi.
I played a barfly and would be rapist,
comically cast without need to audition.
She ran sound,
held boom mikes, rolled tape,
and kept quiet on the set.

Some positions perplexed her
and condoms confused.
Face planted in pillow,
her posterior presented,
she would constantly chatter,
"like this, or like that?"
Riding on top
she'd slide suddenly sideways
and I'd have to remind her
that boners don't bend.
Perusing the prophylactic
she would question
its size, shape and substance.

The rape scene ran everyone ragged
jokes and jests were rampant
and kept the actors sane.

During a long set up
I confided in the sound op,
I'd had sex, sure, but never a girlfriend,
I freakishly found sex and friendship
completely incompatible.
After a long day, she suggested a date.
I smiled and shrugged,
"Only for sex."
She said that would be swell.

As I descended toward her center
she held my head
and told me I didn't need to.
" . . . but what if I want to?"
There was no reply as I began
to nuzzle and nibble, lick and lap.
Her hands flew spastic
not knowing where to rest,
her legs rose once then lay limp
until she savagely bumped and bucked.
She shouted, "What the hell just happened?"

One rainy weekend, months later,
I arrived home and my ragged roomie
slurped his ramen and mumbled,
"Some rat faced girl was looking for you."
I had no clue and little curiosity
as to who this had been,
until he retrieved a familiar phone number.

His insult towards her made me wax weird.
I could see why he said it,
but it couldn't have occurred to me on my own.
I realized that maybe I'd missed more.

Mentally surveying our sex scene,
I felt that if I wasn't her first
I was certainly close.
With her beauty slighted
and her inexperience made plain
I puffed up protective
and padded off to her place.

Comely in a kimono, she welcomed me warmly.
She sat me down sweetly,
and proceeded to praise me.
"Your cosmopolitan attitude has given me courage."
I laughed at the description,
but she pressed on.
She now dated regularly,
where she hadn't before.
She had called up to tell me
what a good deed I'd done.
I blushed and I stammered,
then laughed when I said,
"I'd be glad to do good
if that's all it took!"

Call Me Paco!

It was a hell of a party.
I trip over barbed wire
still hung-over from "The Blood of Iraq".
What the hell did we put in that drink?
I scutter and stumble through butt filled bottles
while straw filled corpses, stolen from protest rallies,
stare and mock insensibly.

Desert Storm had just begun
and a knee jerk contrarianism
caused us to celebrate.
I agreed with the protestors
but it's good to press buttons.
There's nothing better than an evening of alcohol and arguments,
but the aftermath was ugly and I need fresh air.

Dull January light hits my eyes
as I stumble down my apartment stairs.
A car horn hits my ears
and the parking lot jumps at me.
A mind-bending monstrosity screeches to a halt,
battered Cadillac covered in fringe,
with an oddly sexy Virgin Mary on the dash.

"Fuck! Neil, are you all right?"
Cartoonish and a little crazed looking,
a cholo, as reimagined by a Minnesotan housewife,
greeted me from under a spectacularly blue bandana.
"Sayeed, is that you?"
"Call me Paco! The local rednecks will be after Palestinians
now that the war has started."
I laugh until it hurts
and try to tell him he ought to fear the local Mexican population.

Maps

It began before memory,
with the almost sound
of crayons on rough brown paper.
Triangle trees for forests,
and rivers little more
than waving blue lines.

My first friend,
our parents argue
over when we'd met
but when talking of toddlers
it's easier to say
we'd known each other
our entire lives.

Scented magic markers
create more colorful
and complicated
compositions.
Islands outlined
and populated with primitives
and a bevy of wild beasts.

Brother in all but name,
we seldom attended school together.
The vagaries of gifted student programs
kept me matriculating
at different institutions every year,
but our bond was unbroken
I could always rely on him.

The symbology became
more sophisticated.
Cities were located,
mountains measured,
and ocean depths plumbed.

The pencil, t-square and compass
became the tools of the day.

College came
and distances became greater
but we always returned.
Inevitably we were each other's best men
at each other's less than inevitable weddings.
Time proved me mercurial,
angry young man and charitable volunteer,
poet, professor and private eye,
day laborer and drunk.
My friend seems the same
within or without time,
soft-spoken, kind and gentle
competition irrelevant
as he pursues his passions
with a patience profound.

The computer now serves
the cartographer's art,
all forces are factored in
from plate tectonics
to climate change
and a press of a key
will move land masses
with the fictive passing of time.

My friend has a secret,
not a vice, shame,
or other venality,
but merely a private passion
that others aren't likely
to appreciate.
His mother, myself
and likely his bride
are the only ones
who know
who've seen
the worlds within his mind.

He makes maps,
of unseen, unknown
and unknowable places.
They molder in attics and basements,
carefully collected
from four year old's fantasy
to real estate agent's
hidden hobby.
He's always been making them
and he always will,
for himself alone
with no need for others
to bear witness
to their perfection.

I often muse,
that if there are worlds to explore
after ours has expired,
then the gods will surely
find their blueprints
with him.

No Neverland for Wendy

I.

Intercourse interrupted
candle flame flicker from
door swinging draft.
The silhouette is short,
newsboy cap over wire rimmed frames
one lens blackened
to hide a misshapen eye,
a bucktoothed countenance
atop a fragile body
as asexual as a kid's show mascot.

I pause from pleasurable pounding,
Lisa looks back at me
from over her sculpted shoulder.
"Let Wendy watch,
it's all she's got."
Too drunk, damaged and damned to turn back now,
I put Lisa through all the positions left in me,
until we collapse in sweaty release
and the shadowy figure
creeps quietly away.

II.

I worried over Wendy,
the shy roommate of my sometimes squeeze
was seriously fucked up.
There were problems with her pineal
and at the tender age of twenty
she had not
and never would

reach puberty.
She was going blind
and had more conditions and syndromes
than I could count.
Unsurprisingly,
this also wired her weird
and made a mess of her mind.

According to Lisa,
Wendy was more social
whenever I was around.
She painted me pictures
and waxed wondrous
about fantasy and science fiction.
After some quiet consultation
we felt we should take Wendy
with us to a party or two
as a nudge towards normalcy.

Beer brained and relaxed,
heavy with hubris,
I felt the proud poppa,
to see Wendy wander the room
chattering like a chipmunk
to many a broadly beaming partygoer.
Solidly in my own booze groove,
I never noticed when Wendy imbibed.
Mixed with her meds,
the forbidden fruit of alcohol
worked wicked wonders
on her sad and stunted system.

Towering atop the table,
bottles, caps and cups
clattered to the floor

as she jumped up and down.
Then Wendy screamed,
"Why won't someone fuck me?
I'm a virgin
and anyone will do!"

I feel better about humanity
for the fact that no one laughed.
I grabbed Wendy in a fireman's carry
while she fought ferret like for her freedom.
Once at their apartment,
Wendy winged her way to bed,
Lisa became lachrymose,
and I scurried my way elsewhere.

III.

Dull and dreary days later,
Lisa dialed me up for dinner.
The meal was marvelous,
but after dessert
Lisa pleaded her plan
for sexual social work on my part.

I'm sorry to say, but it is here
that I wish I acted differently
or had any sort of tale to tell,
but I became a craven coward
and disappeared,
ditching the drama entirely.

Ah Wendy,
dear Wendy,
I wish you well,
but I never could have done it.

Conquest

With the braggadocio of a self-proclaimed god
I announce to the pool playing drones
"I'm gonna break that girl!"
A tap and a stroke, I turn and am faced with the woman in
question.
She rises in both beauty and stature
and presents me with a sloppy, but controlled kiss.

The scoundrel with his best friend's girl,
I was in a pleasant nightmare
constructed by James M Cain and David Goodis.
A shift in aesthetic styles would confirm my fate.

Betrayal hung malodorously about us,
swamp gas waiting for the match to be struck.
I took note as she bedded the entire outer circle of my
acquaintance.
My friend had her time,
the rabble had her body,
but I had her mind
and I intended to make the most of it.

Red & Green for the Christmas party
A skin-tight red dress and an olive drab military jumpsuit
She hung from me like spanish moss
tight, but able to swing with every passing breeze.

The festivities cut short
by the diamond hard grip of the cuckhold upon my bicep
whirl, stumble, trip and the slam of a backroom door.
"Yeh know tha' yeh're mah verrrrry bes' fren'."
I stifled a laugh at the sad Irish accent he adopts when drunk,
although Lord knows I probably sounded as bad.
He pleaded and warned,
I denied and promised,
and everything was copacetic
for at least the next three hours.

I slept the sleep of the innocent, the just, and the horribly inebriated.
The whisper slide of my bedroom window returned me to consciousness.
She leapt into my room, an avatar of Bast,
pure animal assault on puritan morality.
Warm Egyptian eyes flashed in an icy Nordic countenance.
The moist pads of her fingertips silenced my half-opened lips.
Naked and slowly gyrating in the moonlight,
she caressed my face and played with the hairs on my chest.
In whispers and growls,
sighs and wails,
she recited from Blake's Songs of Innocence and Experience,
and I knew who was really in control here.

Charity Case

Forever consoling, commiserating, comforting
the consummate social worker
she regularly visits the vainglorious I.

A malignant, cancerous drunk
I spread throughout her life for weeks
before dropping my disease.

"So what do you think of me?"
she asks, plaintive, quiet & drunk as well.
"I don't think of you."

Stunned verbal silence as John Zorn creates beautiful sonic
atrocities
When the music fades a duet of nervous laughter ensues.
I explain the ill-conceived non-joke to no-one's satisfaction.

A chaste drunken embrace leads to a chaste drunken coma.
In the morning, I devote a brief moment to self-loathing,
until I realize that she will be back next week.

Galaxy Bowl-a-Rama

Pop culture product of the space race,
its street side sign plucks patrons
a neon powered rocket roars towards
a baffling bowling ball moon.

Once a bastion of blue collar boys
a swaggering salon of beer belch bravado
league night naughtiness meant a welcome reprieve
from wives and witless rug rats

Now a borderline business
making ends meet in the margins
it caters mostly to kids and angsty teens
too young to go blotto in bars.

Italian Boxer

The trailer home sagged to the side of the campground.
A bit of the American mid-west
lost and discarded ten miles from Pompeii.
I sat in my tent and stared at this unexpected sight.

A summer romance had soured,
and here I was acting the archeologist
with her female friends.
That night, the girls giggled and were gone
off to find handsome foreigners to fuck.
Some nights I'd chaperone,
but my self imposed celibacy
made me cranky.
So I drank Cynar and stared
at the dilapidated domicile.

An elderly man emerged
ropey muscled and beaming benevolence
Bob Hope as bruiser.
He rounded the trailer
and pulled pole-mounted punching bags
from behind his home.
I silently rose and helped hoist the heavy bag.
He smiled and set the speed bag up.

Without a word, he held the heavy bag
as I hit it hard.
Soon I was striking for speed
and he smiled as I sweat.
Heart rate high, breath heaving heavy
I sat as he set up more Cynar.

We drank, deeply and long
and conversed
through my high school Latin,
his eight words of English
and plenty of pantomime.

The archeology student and the retired pro boxer,
The pretentious poet and the World War Two vet.
We laughed at unintelligible jokes
and cried at barely understood bathos.
I dropped dead drunk,
head on the picnic table.

Several shrieks in the morning
meant the girls made it back.
They had brought temporary boyfriends,
but the boys had beaten it
along with bags and packs.
I moved maddened
seeking my supplies,
but the boxer brought over my backpack
while rolling his eyes at the hysterical hens.

Root Beer

Tiny bubbles burst
in water sweetened
with sarsaparilla
eliciting childish joy.

Dad and I
have always shared
a peculiar passion
for the simple pleasures
of soda pop.
My childhood was filled
with seltzer water gourmandism.
Every flavor
was sampled and savored,
from classics like Coke and Pepsi
to the more exotic flavors
of birch beer or Cel-ray.
Many a little league loss
was eased
by chasing down
the old school soda fountains
where the syrups
were hand mixed
and the flavor combinations
were limitless.

After
the candy colored luster
of childhood had faded
we both retained our
soda pop love.
Although Dad's diabetes
made him drink diet.

During the bad years,
the sad years . . .

my first fiancée
left me
we overcame
her drug dependency
and she needed me no longer . . .
my friends made the marriage rounds
and each and every new wife
had her new hubby
ditch the drinking buddy . . .
my writing weakened
and workplace worries grew . . .

Then,
one significantly silent birthday
my Dad darkened my dusty doorway
and piled high my sorry studio
with boxes of root beer.
A&W, ICW,
Dad's, Mug, and Barq's
Thomas Kemper,
Dr. Brown's,
Sioux City,
and many more
from all across the world.
I was too moody
to carry on a conversation
but Dad suggested
I gather my friends
for the finest root beer tasting
ever held.
I smiled, nodded
and mumbled my thanks
as Dad departed.

Weeks went by,
and I never found
a single soul
to share
the sweet, simple and silly
pleasure of a root beer fest.

41

After a booze filled bender
I finally cracked
the first root beer bottle
open,
and just as
the caramel colored liquid
was about to hit my lips
I started to cry,
at the knowledge
that the childlike joy
my father hoped to inspire
would not come to pass.

The karmic wheel turns
and my life is full
of friends and family.
My passion for pop
has never diminished,
but root beer
always tastes
a tad like disappointment.

The tiny bubbles bite
in water soured
beyond sarsaparilla's ability
to make things right again.

FELI SNAVIDAD

The S slid across the sign
storm blown
and slick with sleet

The store front is dark and dusty
Its last hoorah the holiday
long past

Generic well wishes
from a failed franchise
now distorted

No one noticed
the failing hope
to press on one more year

Institutional Comforts

I no longer know
the proper euphemism
for nut houses
insane asylums
and mental institutions
but I've visited plenty.

Jessi was a friend's fiancée
badly bi-polar
depression meant suicide attempts
manic meant sexual compulsion.
Once when Up
she stabbed my friend
for thwarting
her desired DP.

Matt was a neighboring peer
post high school, he vanished
for four years, we wondered
suddenly surfacing
living on the beach
no money, no job
few drugs, little speech
somehow, at sometime
he simply stopped
caring.

Courtney was a casual fling
she loved libertinage
she craved cocaine
pursuing a porn career
seemed satisfactory
Her family had money
and felt her choices
meant madness.

I visited them all
different times
different towns
each was unhappy
but had one comfort
not found on the outside.

"At least they let us smoke as much as we want, without giving us
any shit."

The Cynic: a Parable

I met Diogenes once, as he roamed the Earth looking for an honest man. We sat down and I told him of my life. His wizened face bore a near vertical smile as he told me that I may be what he had been looking for. I was overwhelmed with pride, so much so that I scarcely noticed as he began to fondle himself. The sound of his ejaculate hitting the cuff of my jeans startled me out of my reverie. I must admit I lost my head a bit. Before my senses could register the action, I had dealt the old man a crushing blow to the face. In a surge of compassion or guilt, I knelt beside the fallen figure. His arms reached out to me and in stunned silence I allowed him to pull my head forward and place his bloodied lips against my cheek.

He whispered to me, "The honest man lacks mystery, and thereby respect. People desire suspense. The honest man can only destroy, for the world is made of lies. The honest man will never be able to attain anything useful or pleasurable. He is suited only to be a philosopher."

I pulled away from his corpse, newly cognizant of a burden that had always existed. I have walked ever since with traces of impatience in my every movement, insolence in my gaze, and a furrowed brow that envenoms my countenance. I seek but one honest man.

The Lie You Told Yourself

It's made of
the rotten heart meat of over-exposed sorrows
and the coppery blood
of tongues bitten in suppressed anger.

Used as a salve
you slather it on thick
covering picked over wounds.
It lubricates, too.
Allowing you to slither
past unacknowledged fears.

It blends in easily,
unnoticed until you reach for a dream
and it slips through your oily grasp.
The lover leaves.
The career is denied.
Only on those moments
when you are alone
can you come clean.

You can reach for a tool
to scrape the muck free.
Nietzsche's razor blade solace
through the long dark night,
or Epicurus' warm ray of delight
melting icy inhibitions.
But tools only work
at the points where they touch.

When you've uncovered yourself
and squeezed out the pus,
let the sun burn the filth
and the moon kiss your skin,
you just may have the chance
to grasp the next dream.

Conspire

We breathe together

infant gasp in response
to brief slap
while mother pants exhausted

lovers inhale each other's
fevered exhalations
with limbs united even closer

grandfather's death rattle
after three years of chemo
comes as a contented sigh

From Lebanon to Madagascar,
Malaysia to Canada, humanity conspires
against entropy and non-existence

We breathe together

Sincere

A notice to all shoppers:

The clay vessel of my Word
is without wax.
There is no false glue
hiding cracks and chips.
My love is pure and untainted
by the atmosphere.
My hatred is contained
and watertight.
My Word can be seen
to hold any sentiment faithfully,
without wax.

Are you buying?

Colophon

The Last Word
is seldom the writer's.

The publisher's mark,
a brand upon the herd
on which they support
themselves

An ending note
in tribute to
burly men at printing presses

Most often the Last Word
is a rejection slip.

Her Smile was so Seductive

He was compulsed, repulsed and drawn back again
His feelings were unique
never experienced before
and certainly
never to be experienced again

thirty two perfect pearls
opalescent beauty
Abraham's objects of great price.
If He sowed them like Nestor did at Thebes,
what wonders would grow?
Poe's Berenice was grinning again.
He would pursue their whiteness
as Ahab did his whale

He gave up
gave in to his urges
and now
her teeth are rattling
in an old mint tin
mementos
of the one
that didn't get away.

Lizard in a Woman's Skin

Venus in furs
struggles down the corridor
of ecstatic flesh,
falling forward
into silk sheets
and Sapphic bliss.

Her neighbor holds
cocaine fueled orgies.
The noise hides
murder born of shame,
as the sharp steely
phallic substitute
makes new orifices
in which to rest.

Venus rises
as red haired hippies
make murder too.
She blames
her secret self
and drags her family
down.

Father's brains
scooped out with lead,
a weight less than
his fear.
Her daughter dies
as she has lived
hedonism's bill
come due.

Only her husband
carries on
and wanders the streets
seeking
strange meat.

Sub Plot

Leather mask clad geek chic
darling of the dungeon crawl
you're the most sought after slave
in the local S & M scene

Scrubbing down the Sybian,
you sulk savagely behind the ball gag.
Your mad Mistress declared a moratorium
on the swapping and sharing of slaves.
The prospect of boot polishing monogamy
drags you down.

You dare to dream of different doms
while cooking candy for kitschy kink.

Hitchcock schemes come half hatched,
and soon pretty poison,
meant for rodent removal,
is dissolving in delicate drops
of creamy caramel.

"Beg for it, Bitch!" she screams,
as you yawn
and make mechanical motions
of shackle bound
whip writhing.

There is a pregnant pause
as the witch makes you wait.
You glance up and peek peripherally,
witnessing the woman
prematurely pop the cooling caramels
past her ruby red lips.

You cry and cajole,
sob, shake and shudder,

begging her to free you
from your fetters.
"That's more like it!" she mutters
before dropping dead,
a foul froth around her mouth.

Now you slouch sadly
and sob silently
in the sound proofed
dungeon.

Comfort in Cold Flesh

The midnight meat wagon made its way to the morgue
Big-eyed Billy crawled from cot to concealed corner
The entranced observer absorbed orderlies moving masses.
The cold room clicked shut as the boy bobbed over brazenly

Siren's song
of forbidden fruit
singed synapses
sang symphonies
behind Billy's
sallow skin

Single mom surreptitiously secreted son while lingering in the lab
Billy was supposed to slumber soundly in the break room
but boredom begat bravery among the scent of blood and bleach.
Such sights he saw, scared him servile and scarred him sexually

Shotgun suicides
and burned babies
gave goose bumps
but breath-stilled beauties
wired Billy weird

Now a mature mortician mired in Milwaukee
he watches and waits for intact innocents and icy ingénues
to lay luxuriantly among coffins and curtains
until silent satiation stills his horrid hunger

He heaves
corpse compliant
and lets loose
liquid life
in demure death

Shub-Niggurath

Pagan fertility goddess perverted,
the black goat dwells in the wilds,
surrounded by her teeming thousands of children,
writhing in debased mother worship.

Puritan fathers tried to prevent her fecundity,
but they confused sex with evil
and imprisoned love and beauty
while the she-goat's genitals
continue to drip
children malformed from disease.

One day the stars will be right,
and the sleeper will awake
to find the world overrun
by the children of abused nations.
Shub-Niggurath will gurgle her obscene pleasure
as they rend the veil
of our tinsel town reality.

The King in Yellow is Alive and Well

Lovecraft's oldest fear fails to hold its grip
on emo kids, parish priests, or plastic porn stars.
The unknown seems knowable,
and the black gulfs of infinity
have been lit by the neon glow of strip malls.

Worm flesh molded in the form of man,
the King's subjects no longer haunt graveyards.
Their boneless bodies now serve in boardrooms,
discussing defense contracts while eating catered carrion.

The tree of life, be it Sefirot or Yggdrasil,
stands poisoned above Herne's corpse.
Moon touched and greased by gold,
our modern burgomasters blame the tree
for fouling its own foliage.

Bloody Ares grins as Eris sows discord,
for wars are waged as always,
save for the King's innovation.
War spawns death, and death spawns worms
but human faced they're recognized no longer.

The King in Yellow once depended on poets and on playwrights,
but his masked face now whispers into Rupert Murdoch's ears.
For news now entertains, and entertainment is news
and no priest or teen or peasant need see a war child's tears.

Wake Up

Even as they open
your eyes recoil
fearing the responsibility
of a world without excuses.

Your day becomes
a series of calculations
on how to get the sweetest fruit
with the least amount of effort.

Occasionally you stop to stare
at your own amoebic features
reflected back to you
on screen, tube and monitor,
pseudo pods writhing in self-embrace.

Your pleasures exist in some shining void
that separates the dangling objects of desire
from the dusty necropolis of your intellect.

Look down at your hands!
White-knuckled, they clench a weapon
while somewhere people are harvesting
the food that sustains you.

A World of Shit

Zambian child soldier,
painfully hungry
after burning the village,
he once ate
a piece of charred meat
handed to him
by his squad leader.
The giant of a man,
whose presence
radiated strength,
laughed at the speed
in which the flesh
was devoured.

"Little cannibal,
you are now the white man's
waking nightmare."

His old name's lost,
Little Cannibal
will have to do.
Merely eleven years old,
he can't wait
to be old enough
to get the first pick
of available chemical
recreation.
The Qhat and crystal
go fast,
so it's glue or Jenkem
for the little ones.

He defecates
a malnourished
yellow glop

into a plastic bag
containing sugar
and yeast.
A few days in the sun
and the Jenkem
will be ready.

Leaning against
the only wall standing
amidst newly grown jungle,
Little Cannibal
spies a curious creature
from a world
unfathomable.
The English journalist
asks why he would
huff from a bag
of shit.

Such an obvious question
confuses,
so he answers,
"the glue makes me dizzy,
Jenkem gives visions,
I see my dead mother."

Another inhalation
of his own odor
altered by
fermentation,
and the boy
falls asleep
wondering
how many men
the journalist
must have killed
to reach such an age.

Saint Malverde

Prayer cards plastered
about the cockpit,
and the Cessna purrs
under the radar
across the border.

Jesus Malverde,
a charismatic campesino,
came down from the mountain
and traded his machete
for a pistol.
Jesse James
and our man Jesus
made their bones
and reaped their reputations
in the same generation,
albeit on separate sides
of the border.
The impoverished
rooted for them
like Robin Hood,
although they never
seemed to get around
to giving their gains
to the poor.

A short-runway savant,
the pilot pauses
to kiss the saint medallion
before braving
a landing
on a mere three hundred feet
of meadow.

There is no sin in Sinaloa
save having no money,

so when a pistol packing peasant
made pesos a plenty
bleeding avaricious Dons dry,
the people prayed
when he passed
and suggested sainthood
to a nonplussed Church.
The petition rejected,
the Chapel of St. Jesus Malverde
was built without Rome's gold
on the blood and sweat
of the destitute and desperate.

One hundred fifty years later,
the pilot takes a recreational toot
for a job well done
no DEA or double crossing dealers
just a simple transaction
smooth as silk.
On the return trip
he utters a prayer of thanks
to the only soul in Heaven
he knows would understand.
St. Jesus Malverde
Patron saint of drug smugglers

TAP TAP TAP... Move Along

After thirty long years on the force,
Lonnie still prowls the park for perps.
Attempting to end all the drugging and mugging
leaves little mark on Lonnie,
but rousting romantics and laying into lovers
causes a quivering in his quietude.

Lonnie'd been a lonely lad,
sexuality blooming late and lackluster,
until ensconced in armor of blue
he finally wooed and won a woman.
After all these years,
she's still his winsome wife
and keeps home and hearth a happy one.
A darling daughter exists as well
and makes his future palatable.
In all, a life lived safe and sound,
save for a job which makes him tremble.

Shrub shenanigans, and bush balling pervs
mean no more to him than muggers,
gay men he sends upon their way
smiling slightly at their sadness,
but creeping up on rocking cars
seems to shake his soul loose.
The endless, moaning moment
before he taps the glass
is spent in careful watching
the mind of womankind to reveal.

Through foggy windows and tree-lined night
he frets over female faces.
In the gasping and panting of a favored few
he sometimes spies a lamp-lit love
and wanders away consoled.
In the faces of other feverish females
he looks straight into lust

and carries out his duties
content that desires need be chained.
But more and more he finds
the faces that give him fear,
the gape mouthed, blank eyed
vacuum visaged sight
of girls who feel nothing.

Behind the badge, he trembles
at the notion that sex means nothing
to the nubile nudes
in carnal car embrace,
and as he taps upon the glass
and mumbles "Move along"
he suspects they wear the face
of every female everywhere.

Tonight,
a Cadillac seems to jump with joy
as Lonnie creeps beside it.
He quickly spots the waxed mask look,
the specter of indifference
on the countenance of a centaur.
A woman straddled atop her man,
one beast, one body,
and the lower half good only
for perambulation.

Lonnie weeps for base biology
and the myth of making love,
he fingers his revolver
wondering where to send the bullets.
He wants to wash away the coldness
from the face of Aphrodite,
but before firing at the female
fleeting thoughts of wife and daughter
place the gun to his skull instead.

Murder in the Cathedral

The mystery play is over
the curtains have drawn closed
The Everyman is drunk and bloody
caught stealing the Savior's clothes

Dante bore witness to the crime
Beatrice had led him to it.
Yet blind faith in justice done
could not see him through it.

Milton brought the culprit in
lured forth by promised wealth.
But when the suspect took the stand
he spoke well for himself.

Judge Donne was indecisive
he'd worked with friend and foe.
No verdict to his mind would come
while staring at cloven toe

George Herbert was of but one mind
and talked only of the victim.
No evidence could he provide
but the foe, he could not trick him.

'Twas Blake who hung the jury,
talking equally of lust and love,
he took the suspect's side
yet no lightning struck from up above
and we took it all in stride.

The Mystery play is over,
the Passion play is too.
Art and religion oft do mix
but art illuminates when through.

Wonder's End

The therapist returns today
to the house where she was born
She opens the door to her old bedroom
bedecked with unicorn.
A life spent listening to
the demons of the mind
has left her ill prepared
for what she here will find.
The rainbow bridge has fallen
to Surtur's fiery blade.
The unicorns lie slaughtered
in the enchanted glade.
The virgin that entrapped them
reclines after the hunt
she uses every severed horn
to violate her cunt.
The therapist will return to work
on the next November morn
and every patient that she sees
will seem a unicorn.

Who's Your Daddy?

Emancipated and independent,
she had the papers to prove it.
Sun kissed in a sundress
the sixteen year old stood
silent and still, awaiting my word.
"You're hired," I said.
She rushed to my chair
and I cocked an eyebrow
as Marcia Brady's twin
bussed my bearded cheek.
"I'll never forget you!!
You've given me my first job!"

The law allowed emancipated teens
to suffer an adult work week.
She suffered sweetly.
Cute and coquettish with customers,
but bashfully businesslike behind the counter.
When the black eyes began
she was supported on all sides.
Step-father stalker got stepped on,
but anonymous vigilantism
failed to suffice.

A midnight move to a happier home.
Art school students who strip on the side
made magnanimous roommates.
Three months of rent from me
set her up solid and safe.
Soon after she sent
a Christmas card, chaste kisses, and candy.

Next year brought new drama.
Miss Brady found a beau.
A sexuality once stunted turned supernova.
Co-workers and customers complained.

Entire parties were propositioned
to play with her and her boy.
A pile of pictures were placed on my desk.
Brady in bondage, five boys fondling
there were fists amidst the fucking.

Corporate called for firing.

Delaying for a day,
heart heavy I headed for home.
I should have felt sorrow,
but jeering jealousy jinxed me.
Why wasn't I a propositioned party?
Her face found itself affixed
to the flesh of my female companion
via my fertile and fecund fantasy life.
On the morrow I awoke
unwholesome and unholy.

Called into the conference room,
with witnesses along the wall,
she preempted the proceedings.
Nervous with news and quick to quit,
Marcia would be moving.
Marcia would be married.
While the corporate witnesses
were silently satisfied,
she slipped me a gilded note:

"Would you give me away at my wedding?
You're the closest thing to a father I've ever had."

The Figure on the Threshold

Her name upon my lips,
an invocation to alien divinities
worshipped in secret
here and now.
The silence following her greeting,
knowing she recalls my touch,
a shadow out of time
threatening to swallow eternity.

A beautiful malignancy
rending the transparent veil
of timid domesticity.
I shan't succumb,
acquiesce,
or surrender,
but I may very well
evaporate in the heat
of tempestuous possibility.

Rockin' the Ramrod

Relaxin' with muscle-bound women,
I lounge luxuriant
behind my beer.
The grrrls and I
sit in unspoken social segregation,
lesbians only linger
in the quietest corner
of the gay bar.

Midweek, mid-afternoon business is barren,
but a knot of himbos congregate
by the bathroom
and begin the great debate
over whether I'm gay
or whether I'm straight.

"That looks like a twink punching bad boy."
"Dude, I know that knuckle dragger,
he's breeder to the bone."
" . . . but he's the beariest bear
I want to see bare!"

A leather clad Leroy
has had enough nonsense
and ambles over to ask,
"Straight boy,
don't you have enough
sports bars to hang in?
Why do you have to hang here?"
Feeling too hollow to get hostile,
I try to explain
that this bar has the best
drink deals downtown,
but before
I put wind to my words

the shaved headed pixie beside me
tries hard to be tank girl's twin
and aggressively utters,
"He's with us."

After the interruption,
I order a round for the table,
and give the grrrls grief
for their demure drinking style.
Challenged to show how it's done,
I give lessons in chugging down brew.
The secret lies in training your throat
to stay open
and not gag,
then you can polish off a pint
in one swig.

My lesson must have been loud,
because the knot of boys
stared, laughed lascivious
and opined about the wonders
of an eagerly open throat.
I laughed back,
lit and sucked the smoke
from a lengthy cigar.
They nearly drowned in drool
as I elbow nudged
my friend Martha,
"Is this how it feels to be a cock tease?"
"How the hell would I know?!"

We held out through happy hour,
but began to roll out
before the meat market began in earnest.
As I shrugged into my jacket,
a crusty fellow
and reputed bug-chaser
sidled alongside and said,
"I like sucking straight boy cock."
"I'm sorry pal,

but it's a full moon in May,
the only time that
Martha likes men
and I'd hate to miss my chance
to have her toss me around."
As we exited,
I proceeded to kiss the she-bear
and giggled as she grimaced.

Throwing Punches

I'd accumulated too much comp time
so they sent me home.
Home smelled of cooking oil,
it had spilled off the coffee table,
it glinted off my girlfriend's generous ass
and the cock of the man
buried deep in it.

She was sandwiched between
would-be rock stars from next door.
One administered a fleshy colonic
while the other choked her
and spit in her face.
Remarkably unsurprised
I watched for a moment
my head tilted
like a dog
attempting algebra.

Mere moments produced
Slack-jawed stares and
insincere apologies.
"Get out of my apartment!"
They were sent scrambling
after jeans, shoes, and jackets.
Slicked down weasels ran
bare assed down the hall.
I had paused
only to grab her key
and send her sprawling as well.

I should have seen it coming.
The babe had been bitching
that I hadn't hit her hard enough
or wrecked her, rough and raw.

This required further thought,
so I wandered to the worst watering hole
I could find.

Past the peep shows,
the Mirror tavern sat
selling slow suicide
to any and all.

An ancient Indian,
one-armed and wasted,
would throw
periodic punches
at any white man
that didn't patronize the place
regularly.
He ignored me that evening,
and I knew I was now a member
of an exclusive club
in hell.

Drinking rat water gin
I pondered past punches.
Getting hit
reminded me
of Jorge Martinez
attempting to
bash my brains out with a brick.
Hitting
reminded me
of Lucas Hopperstadt
weeping out "why?"
as he doubled over
from my blows.
I wished neither bad memory
associated with my sexuality
and so I had disappointed my darling
when she wished it rougher.

A dozen drinks down
and I wondered
why I had never found
a quiet cutie
who regularly read
Austen and Elliot.
But my ruminations were ruined
by the booth behind me.

Three samples of
white collar machismo
gone slumming in this saloon.
They dug the dive scene
and double dog dared each other
to endless acts of stupidity.

One of them spoke louder and louder,
and grew prouder and prouder,
of his ability to navigate
the lands of the lower class.

"It's all about being aware
and being prepared.
No mugger will strike,
or homie hassle,
if they see you're prepared
and have the muscle."

He wasn't ready for my quick combo.
His nose nearly flattened
under my right.
His lips ripped wide open
from the rings on my left.
A casual graze from a canine
left my fist
covered in my own claret.

No reprisals were forthcoming.
Loudmouth bawled like a baby
while his friends sat silent.

Soon, a wave of dark mirth
erupted from the bar.
The Indian, the pimp,
two whores, and seven sad old drunks
all began laughing
and buying me booze.
In short time, I was sloshed
and grinning like Lucifer
I left for the clubs
to seek a temporary girlfriend.

The evening was still early
and it passed in a haze.
What madness transpired I may never know,
my eyes opened to antiques
and fiercely feminine furnishings,
but my nose smelt rot, death and decay.
My skin felt flushed.
no one answered my calls.
I rose,
a dull throb answered.

Five pounds of raw meat
had replaced my left hand.
Malodorous Pus oozed
from a tiny hole
where the tooth had grazed it.

Passing out,
my eyes rolled
in an attempt to see my own brain.
I was certain my sins
had collected in my fist.
I could only hope
my unknown hostess
would save me.

Rescue

It was three days after the argument.
A moderate fuss, in which I suggested
her continued baiting of her ex
to be unhealthy.

Her reply?
That I was jealous
and not appropriately grateful
for her attentions.

Three days of unanswered calls,
(only two a day, for I am a patient
and temperate man)
and the worry set in,
and the real calls began.

To a mutual friend: she had not been seen
To a co-worker: absent for days and likely to be fired
To her Mom: a new torrent of worry

I recruited my acid-scrambled roomie,
a feral chicken of a man,
for a drive to her apartment.
It was midnight
and the drones were all sleeping.

Lights on,
human barks heard from the street.
I moved, curb to stairs to door
in time-stilled fear.

The door opened of its own will
on the studio turned prison.
Rock-a-billy orangutan standing guard,
red-eyed and crystal crazed

"Wha'choo want, faggot?"
The words hit my ear
as his greased head hit my stomach.
Why must I start all my fights from the floor?

She screamed from the corner
all heaving bosoms, red hair, and long legs
No fierce femme fatale,
but cinema's good girl in the final reel.

My head hurt horribly,
being pounded on the hardwood.
Soon his thumbs were in my eyes
until saw-toothed and angry
one of them was in my jaws.

An eccentric affectation,
I wore a railroad spike
on a leather thong
dangling from my belt.

At some point,
the spike was in my hand
and then his head
and then his head

The feral chicken shrieked, "Police!"
A blur of blood bolted
Occipital bone broken
I collapsed before bureaucrats in blue

I kept clothes soaked with my foe's blood
until hygiene overcame machismo
I kept the girl for years
until I understood
that this was a prologue
of my life to come.

Angie's Advice Often Goes Unheeded

Squat cinderblock building
neon sign outside
the name, Angie's, lit in blue
shooting through a glowing red star
underneath
unlit
it reads:
Bail Bonds.

A big bellied, hairy knuckled brute,
Angus Thermopyle
leans back in his chair
feet on his desk
and smokes a huge cigar
as I walk in.

I once asked him
about the name on the sign.

His reply was simple.
"The Wops call me Angie.
The Wops make up most
of my clientele."

I tell him my latest tale of woe.
With lazy competence,
calls are made
and papers signed.
My errand accomplished
I pause to gripe
about the paucity
of my pocket book.
Angus nods,
points to posters on the wall,
"You could always find freaks for me."

I linger
longer than I intended.
After a moment or two,
Angus opines,
"I say this to women
more often than guys,
but if you have to visit me
this often,
then your spouse ain't worth it."

I sulk in silence,
accept his proffered cigar
and watch
teasing tendrils of smoke
escape skyward.

Leaving New Jersey

Having sex this morning was unexpected
and angry.
My wife's hips seemed to stab me
as she responded to my every thrust.
She is back to sleep already,
unemployed and unhappy.
A stare at her rat's nest of red hair
as I put on my Harris tweed jacket.
(The leather patches on the elbows
help others see my professorial credentials).
She's been clean for over a month this time,
but I wonder just what I'll return to
when the MLA conference is over.

I stride purposely down the squalid apartment steps.
There's a mob scene in the lobby
as police wrestle a figure from the apartment office.
A lanky Serb in janitorial coveralls,
the superintendant moans in basso profundo,
and forces the cops to drag dead weight.
Glimpsed in brief, the open office door
offers the sight of hundreds of roaches covering a lumpy tarp.
I edge out the back door by the laundry room
and the sights of South Orange greet me.

The homeless gossip as well as anybody
and four or five street regulars ask about my apartment.
Uncharacteristically, I brush them off
and head to the train station.
I'm Boston bound then headed to Harvard,
someone seems to want my opinion on
"Monk" Lewis and Anne Radcliffe.

Too painful to look at my presentation yet again,
I instead grab a cheap sci-fi novel
and dream of sojourning among the stars.

Somewhere in Connecticut I wonder
if I really need to return to New Jersey.

Twitch and Froth

The head and feet twitch
tapping,
staccato
on the linoleum.
When the froth
from her lips
covers
the diaphanous
vintage nightgown
I know
it's serious

An aficionado of Munchausen
feigning illness
to end an argument
was not
an uncommon
practice for her
but
the drug cocktail
of choice
for today
has reduced her
raw and rabid

We have our own
EMT kit
hospitals mean rehab
as I reach for
the well worn
plastic case
I know
it won't be for the last time
I know
it won't end our love
I know
her denial of it will

I know
when I'm gone
this will happen
again
and again
until she dies

and it did.

Lachrymose

Why cry?
Isn't it akin to baring one's throat
before the pack leader?
an unnecessary vulnerability?
Tears elicit sympathy,
they've won over hearts
cold with life's inevitable defeats.
But isn't that the survival trait
of prey?
Is weeping a balance?
An evacuation of Galen's melancholic humour,
that if held within
would kill the subject with despair?
Could that ancient doctor have been right,
when he was wrong about so much else?
These salty drops of liquid
are a genetic memory
of a time when sorrow
meant the present threat of physical danger,
and a quick flood of cleansing tears
meant clearer vision and a greater chance of survival.
If only these tears
granted clearer vision
today.

Broken Conscience Interrogation

Why lie
about your loss of employment,
when your wife will
certainly suspect something?
The victim of burst bladder politics,
your workplace rivals
delayed your decision making ability
until any proposal proved
too little, too late.

Why cry
when your reluctant return
from the office
reveals an unsuspected infidelity?
After witnessing your one love
pleasure the postman,
your tears only provoke
lewd laughter at the spectacle
of a soul in decline.

Why try
to reign in the rage,
when the marble based lamp
feels so good in your hands
and better upon their
eggshell skulls?
There are plenty of pills
to offer relief
in the afterglow
and aftermath.

Why die?

Making Time with Hera

I place an acorn
on my windowsill
to keep the lightning out.
Zeus is no friend of mine
for I've been making time
with his wife.

O, maligned Goddess of fidelity,
how could you turn Zeus a cuckold,
against thy very virtue?
I'm no preening Adonis
to win a woman's gaze
against her will.

Is it simply that faith rewards the faithful?
I've lit votives on your dusty altars,
while even Poseidon ravages Medusa
within temples to chastity.

Or perhaps while still pissed at Paris,
you heard me mumble,
Aphrodite may be sexy
but I'm tempted to be true.

But I can't worry about the why,
when there's pleasure to be had
among peacock haunted bowers
where your husband won't hear
for he's too busy
raping women
while posing as a swan.

Splinter

Pulling weeds from amidst the beauty bark,
a bit of wood, dark and sharp
penetrates her pink and tender flesh.

No emergency, but mentioned
in dialogue with her mother.
She gets no aid but a suggestion
to wear gloves next time.

A grimace when she grips
gives her away at work.
Colleagues query why her husband
wasn't pulling the weeds

The injury turns hot and throbbing
infection burrowing deeper than the wood
and old friends find fault
in cheap bark and a lack of tools

Shame faced she finally seeks her spouse.
He drains pus, pulls the splinter
and bandages the wound while saying,
"it's only as bad as you let it be."

Sharking

I couldn't help but stare at that ass
in the Polaroid
on the wall.
That woman's rear was plenty pink,
pleasingly plump,
and perfectly pulchritudinous.
The drool worthy vision was marred
by the aged frat boy
poised and puckered to kiss
the dreamy derriere.

A trophy of sorts,
the picture was pinned
to the pool tournament
bulletin board.
The men's league champ had lost
to the lady's league counterpart.
That kiss didn't seem like much
of a penalty,
but the pic let me know
that I could make money
at this bar.
They'd bet on anything.

I'll pass on the pool tables,
too much true talent out there
and the money was stale.
The newly inaugurated trivia tourney
would best suit my skills,
most of the players' mettle was untested
and a fresh game
always meant more money.

You can't make cash
without a couple of shills,
so I brought along a couple
of bar buddies and pub pals:

Doug's dented head draws stares
at the sign-up sheet,
a tractor accident as a teen
left him seeming simple.
At over 450 lbs,
Sean has trouble finding a seat,
yet won't stop rattling on
about roller-coasters
he'll never be thin enough
to ride again.
They're not fast friends
but as long as I keep
the booze flowing,
they're as loyal
as dogs.

The games begin,
the questions start,
we decide to keep the con simple.
I purposely play pathetic,
confusing Stallone with Willis,
Hemmingway with Gogol,
Doug and Sean hoot and howl
as I lose beggarly bets
to the two.
A little later,
the cash amounts climb
and game gamblers
join our circle.
I let the moneyed suckers
lead early and easy,
coming back in the late rounds
but letting them take
the mid-level stakes.
I cry and cajole,
claim it was close,
and beg for bigger bets,
sensing a sure thing
the suckers set it up
and then the hammer falls.

Catiline conspired
on the Street of the Scythemakers,
Kubrick helmed the Killing,
and Sonny Liston liked leopard skin coats.
People pale at my trivia prowess,
some players are positively apoplectic.
A solid shut-out,
a windfall win,
cash only
no checks.

Sidled up to the bar,
I celebrate with Sean and Doug.
Back from the bathroom,
a red-faced mark
shouts "Shark!"
and seeks to stare me down,
I smile, shrug and
go back to my booze.

It's last call,
and my companions head home.
Pleased with my performance
I'm parking lot bound
when an unseen presence pins me,
then my face to the wall
he kicks my kidneys.
A timely bartender
breaks up the brawl,
and I avoid the sight
of the surly sucker
as I creep to my car
avoiding the possibility
of cops and questions.

The evening's evaluation
at my apartment
reveals a tidy thousand dollars
and the likelihood of pissing blood
for a few painful days.

A typical take,
but perhaps I'd better
wait a week
before attempting
to pad my paycheck
again.

A Job Like Any Other

Itty bitty Betsy
was sexy like a spider,
impossibly thin, all legs and arms
full of elegant angles
and sharp edges,
utterly alien
and yet . . .
and yet . . .
completely compelling
in her skintight suits
of latex or leather.

I winced for her
every time I heard
another alcohol soaked wit
remark
"I'm seeing stars"
while staring at the
astronomical bodies
tattooed atop
her cleavage
as she served them
their beer.
My wince by proxy
was as close
as she ever got
to caring.

The girls always gathered
at my table
on fight night.
Boxing brings out the boors,
but I was always well behaved.
Lori and Amy, Pamela and Stephanie
joked about their jobs
and showed off their new shoes

while I watched
undercard underdogs
punch poetically.
But when Betsy's shift ended
and she brought us all booze,
the tone and tenor
of the distaff conversation
shifted suddenly,
and even I
found eavesdropping
more promising
than pugilism.

The girls were a-quiver
with curiosity
over Betsy's new profession.
A diminutive dominatrix,
her black widow walk
left no doubt
she excelled
in hurling humiliation
and winning worship.
I missed the main event
from straining to listen
as Betsy was quizzed
to the cracking point
by the giddy gynos
at the table.

Betsy confessed
she couldn't stand sex.
No guy or girl
could get her off,
but she sometimes
could help herself
to eye-rolling ecstasy
when fantasizing about
making men miserable
and causing girls to grovel.

Making a job of it,
pleased her personally
late at night
in her inviolate lair,
but the day-in, day-out of it
was a job like any other.

Betsy laughed,
the rustling of husks
drained dry,
as her story ended
and she caught me
hanging on every word
fixated more fiercely
than her actual audience.
Suddenly beside me,
she licked my earlobe
and wanted to know
what I was doing on
Wednesday.

I was single
and certain I could cope
with crazy.
Somewhere, I also suspected
I could save her sexually.
I waited for Wednesday
crafting curious scenarios
suggesting badass
bedroom athletics.

When the time arrived
I rolled downtown
prompt to pick her up.
Layered in latex
she slid into my car,
handed me sap gloves
and a taser,
then presented her proposal:

one hundred an hour
to be her body guard.

So I found myself
smoking a stogie
outside the bedroom
of some nameless nebbish,
shaking my head
at the strange sounds
and unwholesome odors
emanating from within.
I don't know about her gig,
but what I was doing
was indeed
a job like any other.

Skull Shaped Bead

Toe jostled
in the dust and detritus
after the movers have left,
a tiny anchor to a grief
not yet forgot.

Death's head in miniature,
one of hundreds
gifted to us
by my heroin addled,
psilocybin saturated,
mother-in-law.
Reservation raised
and commune created,
she made money
trading in exotic
baubles and beads.

This bead,
once one of those beads,
was made of bone,
human bone,
hand carved
by the lowest castes
along the banks
of the seven holy rivers of India.
They'd sift through the ashes
of fresh funeral pyres
and craft the beads
from the fragments found there,
to sell
as a reminder to the rich
of mankind's mortality.

Nearing my nuptials,
my bride to be
braided
a dozen bone skull beads
into my mane.
I was wed,
kilt clad
and beautifully barbaric,
but it just might be
that those damned beads
symbolized sorrows to come.

Three years in
and the divorce
drained and damaged me.
There were addictions
and accusations,
and although the world
found me righteous
my nest was wrecked
and the feathers that lined it
lost.
How odd then,
that a bag of these beads
followed me.

A buzzing of spiteful
mosquitoes,
there were rumors
of an overdose
and a coma.
I couldn't tell if I cared
and became more confused
as the rumors were confirmed
and my ex-wife's family
played games
over asking me
to the hospital
or later
the funeral.

Not invited to the funeral
I was fine with not attending
but found myself
thinking of my ex
more than I cared to.
A clever cat
and not so secretly spiritual,
I rigged up a ritual
sure to salve my soul
and set my memories at ease.
The beads,
I'd give them away
bit by bit
to friends and acquaintances
and ask them
to make art of it.

The conception
and ceremony
seemed sound,
and I had only asked
for a photo
of the finished product.
Yet few close friends
felt up to the task,
and those farther afield
in my circle
failed me as well.
One dainty dream catcher
the only result of dozens
of potential projects.
Sometimes I daydream
of the beads laying dormant
in desks around the world.

Perhaps it's a more fitting symbol
of my life with her
than I had expected,

potential squandered
and the specter of death
present in every piece.

Toe jostled
in the dust and detritus
after the movers have left,
a tiny anchor to a grief
not yet forgot.
I roll the bead
between shaking fingers
and hurl it
into the dark.

I won't have it follow me
to my new home.

Tedium

a morning spent worrying the bacon fat
from between your teeth.
niggling soreness from a panoply of paper cuts
or a cavalcade of calluses
caffeine, your sole motivator,
has turned on you, tweaking your nerves,
scouring your stomach, and shaking your bowels.

the day will get no better
nor the next
a dead end job the result
of endless personal compromise.
office gossip has soured
newly arrived flesh
no different from the last,
and the eternal question of where
each co-workers' genitals rest
seems like no more than an exercise
in high school geometry

a day is taken off for soul sickness,
spent in a blur of daytime TV
and ladies night at the neighborhood bar.
you return to work unchanged.
your last true vacation long past
now a collection of photos
from a city that seemed
disturbingly like your own.

what now? and where to?
promotion irrelevant and dreams deferred,
you still hope to realize some spark of life
but inertia keeps you still
so you wait for it to come to you.

Exorcism

Steal my eyes and fill my mouth with dirt,
I'm done with being possessed by you.
A Puppet to your phobias and philias,
what crime have I not committed in your name?

You are enslaved to your own master,
but he, they or it means little to me now.
You've spun my head around,
made me blaspheme against my belief,
and sheltered your wickedness in my very flesh.
Control is not yet my own
but I'm not beyond asking for help.

A priestess has arrived,
inverting your gendered expectations.
She feeds me her host and blesses without cost.
Our holy words are our own,
but they chase you away nonetheless.
You've been no more than a spirit for years,
but your fading scream assures me
that now you are even less.

Eccentric Libido

Rah, Rah, Rebellion!
The American Dream
ain't no white picket fence,
everyone here
from banker to butcher,
beauty queen and
JV football hero
has a bone deep belief
in their own rebelliousness.
Three hundred million
James Deans
and Norma Raes
bucking the trends
and fighting the odds
with their own sense of style.

But,
if you want to
lay the lie
to rest,
simply ask them
who they think
is attractive.
Be prepared
for a mind numbing
recitation
of Angelinas
and Anistons,
Depps
and Pitts.
They might as well
be bleating.

Answering the question
honestly,
there've been
accountants and artists,

bartenders and barristas,
even cab driving cuties
who've fired up my loins
far more
than these plastic idols
of the masses.

This is not to deny
my own sycophancy
to celebrity,
but there is no bevy
of Baywatch babes
in my dreams.
Rather,
my nights hold visions
of Tura Satana
stepping
on the back of my neck,
a green skinned
Barbara Steele
offering me a cup
to lap from,
or any of a thousand
more interesting
forms of Venus.

Learning to Dodge Bullets

I.
She caught me skulking beside the bookstore,
another sad sack scoping her out.
The book selling babe
was a Mensa member
with callipygian curves,
she seemed certain
to shoot me down
and mock my awkward gawking.
Before I could begin badinage,
she cradled my crotch
while quietly
inviting me to coffee.

We quaffed caffeine,
cozy on couches.
The subject of sex slid sideways
and careened off the corners
of our conversation.
Something sparked
when I spoke of sex as
transformative and transcendent,
and she declared,
if pregnancy, disease, and social stigma
could be avoided
she would make it her mission
to fuck everyone in the world.

I sat in silent surprise,
as she spun scenarios:
She prophesied a new pedagogy for pubescents
as she loosed lessons in fellatio upon them.
An anarchic angel among ancients
she wanted to recreate the raunchiest
memories of the elderly
and promise new pleasures to old flesh.

She dreamed of dangerous dalliances
with every amateur Adonis and veritable Venus,
to bathe in their beauty
while they wallowed in her worship.
She'd slowly strip for the deaf
and sing her orgasms to the blind.
She wished to experience every ecstasy
of the facile and friendless
and knew they'd be better off for it.

At my quiet query
she tut tutted all taboos
and sought sex with family too.
She craved caresses
from hands that had held
her infant body
and sought sexual congress
with the source of her existence,
both seminal spark
and withered womb.
I accepted the napkin
with her number on it,
even as I struggled
with the image of her head
upon her Mee Maw's lap.

II.
Days went by,
and I didn't dial.
Those digits daunted me,
was I terribly turned on
or trepidatious
over an id unleashed?

When passing the post office
traffic tried to entangle me,
and a back road detour
seemed a solid solution.
Bare skin in a backyard
forced my foot to the brakes.

Vic Hugo noted,
"a naked woman is a woman armed,"
and this sun bathing siren
held a howitzer.
It was the troubling book babe
making Miss Mansfield
look like a lackluster
Olive Oyl.
I transformed into a Tex Avery wolf
and was soon saturated in my own salivation.
Fearful of my potential for foolishness,
I flew home,
but now I nursed a heavy hunger.

Memory fades,
but the digits must have been dialed
and a date was made.
We rolled retro rock-a-billy
and bounced beautifully
into a bowling alley
filled with tiresome teens
too young yet
to meet and mate
in clubs and bars.
We giggled at our own glamour,
debauched gods in a nine lane Olympus.

Although pleased
that this oddball date
had gone pitch perfect,
my soul sickened
as she assured me
her caffeine crazed
sexual soliloquy
was entirely serious.
No psychic, I nonetheless
saw a firm future before me,
filled with drug drama,
jealousy jags,
and arbitrary accusations.

I'd perpetually pursued
bad girls and wicked women,
as a sailor I'd lost many a ship
to a song,
but that night I discovered I need not
and I plugged my ears to the sound.
There was a kiss and a cuddle,
followed by lingering lust
but I went home alone
secure in my new ability
to dodge bullets.

Opera Singer

Tired of tats and tracks,
monogamy scorning polyamorists,
and mandatory creative kink
to keep up my cool credibility.
I said to myself,
"I gotta get me a good girl,
there's no more mileage with the bad."

I knew they were out there,
freethinking good girls
with brains, beauty and guts.
I frequently had female friends
who fit that description,
but the days of daring to date them
were far behind me now
I sought a clean slate,
the dawning of a new day,
etcetera
ad nauseum.

My clever compadres
sought a set-up
and found a fix,
a blind date with a well scrubbed soprano,
timely touring with the opera.
She was bible-belt bred
and Bob Jones raised.
Astute adulthood rejected
wrong-headed righteousness
and ignorant intolerance,
but she retained
an archaic etiquette
and was mindful of manners.
She sought a bashful bohemian,
a prim yet worldly liberal.
Perhaps I'd do.

She was gaga for Greek food
so we met for moussaka.
As she darkened the doorway
she was dressed demurely,
but the largesse of her lung power
was evidenced externally,
D-cups on an A frame.
My unsavory stare
was swiftly dismissed
with a wise witticism on my part
and we sat down to dine.

Time took a vacation
as she eagerly absorbed my every anecdote.
I told of drug dalliances and barroom brawls,
academic achievement
and a deep desire for an artistic success.
Drawing her out was more difficult,
but I can be a lively listener.
At length, she timidly told me
of a life lived in flight,
from a fearful family
and the dangers of her own desires.
She wandered the world lost and lonely,
enveloped in the classical music community
and seldom socializing outside it.

The date ended sweetly,
the taste of baklava
lingering on her lips
as we kissed.
Further assignations followed.
Picnics in parks,
evenings with orchestras
whiled away the weeks.
Feverish carnal fumblings
provided pleasure
and yet never arrived
at their obvious goal.

She phoned
one wet, winter weeknight
as I lay blue-balled
but oddly content.
She'd heard heavy things,
torrid tales of bad behavior.
She said I scared her
and she wasn't certain
I was safe to be around.
This was too silly for me to be stunned.
I couldn't care where
she heard such things.
I did wonder why
she believed them,
but I couldn't be bothered
to figure out the facts
or offer explanations
to charges I didn't understand.

I simply set down the phone,
went back to the bars,
and wondered why it was
I wanted a good girl in the first place.

Fuck Buddies Don't...

I.
She's dead now.

When I met her,
I'd already learned
the hard lessons of my heart,
the soul deep savior syndrome
that led me to dally
with the damaged.
I'd vowed
no more romance
with the wounded,
but slave to my psyche
I still sought to save
and sex was possible
provided the understanding
that nothing deeper
could occur.

From my side of the bar,
I heard the complaints
long before I saw her.
Women whispered words
like skank, slut, and whore,
while the men were mad
that a poor pool player
had taken up too much time
on the tables.

Typically armed with beer and book
I braved the pool room.
Her presence screamed spectacle.
Clad only in a large men's wife beater
and a dainty pair of Doc Martens,
she showed her center
whenever she stretched
across the table to scratch a shot.

Blood red lips on a shaved head
laughed loudly at the grief given
by redneck pool hustlers
angry at her horsing around.
I returned to my reading
and a little writing,
until her improbably purple eyes
caught me smiling at her antics
and she launched herself
into my lap.

"You're the only one here man enough to fuck me."
"I imagine that's true."

We drove back to my place,
passing work lights
in the industrial park.
She sought to shock me
and whispered
that straight sex bored her,
all she wanted was ass
and mouth
and perhaps
some fun with fists.
With eyebrow cocked
I shrugged
and she giggled,
"You'll do just fine."

Five minutes after arriving
at my apartment,
she lay half on
and half off
of my couch,
t-shirt off
and boot clad feet
spread wide,
snoring and perfectly
passed out.

I laughed,
went to my office
and worked on a screenplay
until dawn.

II.
She's dead now.

A couple of weeks went by
without words exchanged
from either direction.
Then . . .
with a bolt of telephonic lightning
she invites me to dinner.

I almost didn't recognize her
as she came to the car
from the coffee shop
where I paused
to pick her up.
She was dressed
in a 1920's idea
of the exotic east,
complete with
a Theda Bara $tyle turban
covering her punkish
shaved skull.

I followed her directions
to a faux Victorian mansion
deep in the woods.
This was not the restaurant
I had been expecting,
but she quieted my queries
with a blow job
while we remained parked
in the circular drive-way.

I spent the evening stammering,
stuttering, and smiling like a simp,

as she introduced me
to her parents, sister, and
other relatives I can't recall.
Feeling awkward and alien,
dinner passed in geologic time,
and when finished
I cornered the comely
agent of chaos
who had led me here.

"My divorce did me in,
I don't do drama,
I'm your friend
and part time fuck,
but I can't be more
than that."

She snorted,
and said I was stupid.
She only wanted
someone stable
to dine with her family
the night before
they forced her
into rehab.

III.
She's dead now.

I wrote to her in rehab.
I wrote of friends
and family
and even
my hard to talk about
ex-wife,
and their experiences
in similar circumstances.
I wrote that the world
could be bigger than
her addictions

or rehab's solutions
if she wanted it to be.

She wrote back,
in a painfully labored
grammar.
Without reading a word,
each unsteady letter
seemed to scream,
"I'm trying my best here."

She wrote of boredom
and secret sexual acts
with tattooed chola.
She illustrated the latter
with comically executed
sketches.
The letters continued
and revealed the boredom
to be true,
but the sex
to be less so.
Ultimately,
she asked me
to pick her up
from the facility
because no one else would.

IV.
She's dead now.

Weeks after her release,
she came to me
and announced
she would be
an actress.
She seemed to treat this
as if she had simply
applied to work
at Starbuck's.

A community theatre
was holding auditions
for a production of
Romeo and Juliet.
She needed me
to make sense of
Shakespeare for her.
Dropping by daily,
without drink, drugs,
or even the suggestion of sex,
she studied hard,
and I was happy
to work in a field
that I had been trained for.

One day,
the dam broke
and her brain
was flooded with understanding.
She felt she could read
any Elizabethan verse
and get it.
Made raccoon-like
by tear traced mascara,
she kissed and hugged me
with great fervor,
before leaving to sign up
for the audition.

I don't know the details,
but she never got the part.
Time tumbled along,
and I seldom saw her,
hearing only
that she now lived with
a Tongan dealer
of crystal and coke,
a man famous for
his ability
to remain motionless.

A rare reading
of a local rag
informed me
she had been picked up
by the police.
I sighed with unsurprise
as I tossed the paper
aside.

V.
She's dead now.

Time taunts and troubles
on occasion,
there's no doubt
that it passed differently
for me and for her
'twixt my reading the paper
and the arrival of the envelope.

It was large,
stuffed near to bursting,
and it had arrived from
the women's penitentiary
in Purdy.
Polaroids poured forth
from the scissor ripped top,
and I paused in worried wonder
knowing that no such package
would be allowed to leave
the prison.
Impossibilities aside
I gathered up her gift.

The photos were artless nudes,
each and every one.
She was emaciated,
with the ribs
of a starving desert dog.

The close confines
and institutional colors
only added to the sense
of dehumanization,
an animal penned.
Her glassy eyes
burned through the film
with cold fire,
while she bent and contorted
in various poses,
seeking to bare her soul
through
gynecological exam.

The short accompanying letter
was sodden with soap opera sentiment,
empurpled declarations of love
and promises to make me happy.
I jumped as if bit,
and feverishly struggled
to quickly write a reply
as if my speed in writing
would be reflected by
the post office.

I hoped what I wrote
was consoling,
commiserating
yet clever enough
to leave her with a laugh,
but most importantly
I hoped
to make it clear
that I was just
a fuck buddy.

Two weeks passed too soon,
and another envelope arrived.
Almost as thick as the one before,

it opened to reveal
sheets upon sheets
of pulp textured paper
scrawled upon
with what seemed to be
charcoal.

A heart rattling list,
it read:

FUCK BUDDIES DON'T
WRITE GIRLS IN REHAB

FUCK BUDDIES DON'T
TEACH SHAKESPEARE TO FUCK-UPS

FUCK BUDDIES DON'T
STAND UP FOR SLUTS IN SPORTS BARS

and on it went
for hundreds of entries.

I couldn't write back,
I'd feel sick when I tried
and the day I heard
of her overdose
I cried for days
upset
at the relief I felt
for not having
to face her.

My Chick

Since relocating rurally
I often find myself frequenting
the farm supply store.
I'm always pleased at the prices
of produce and milk,
but I love to marvel
at their other merchandise.

Over the counter vet supplies
offer plenty of hip kicks
for those in the know.
The unregulated narcotics
kept from recreational use
only by the merchant's whim
and eye for outsiders.

Fast by the freezer
sits a sign advertising semen
for all barnyard types.
The arrested adolescent in me
always needs to
stifle a snicker.

But the big draw,
my personal magnet,
is that container
of condensed cuteness:
the chick hatchery.
Four wooden walls,
a window
a heat lamp hovering
over a hopping horde
of fluffy yellow peepers.

One day my wits will escape me
and I'll purchase my own little peeper.

At home the scramble will start,
while keeping the cat
from my new critter,
I'll ignite the internet with questions
on how to raise the runt.

An unapologetic meat eater,
familiar with killing my own food,
there will be jokes, japes and jests
at my expense
and I will not take them well.
My baby bird will be
first among fowl
and exempt from
the world's wickedness.
From chirping chick
to heavenly hen,
she will be
primped, pampered and preened
my feathered friend
and companion
to an imagined second childhood.
Although this scenario
has yet to unfold,
I write this as a warning.
Should such a thing come to pass,
I will aggressively annihilate
all who may mock
me
or my chick.

The Mythological Urge

On a rainstorm mail run,
I pause by the box,
suddenly aware of being watched.

Dark eyes burning
yet beady,
set deep in a hulking,
feather covered,
totem pole.
Shoulders hunched
against thunder,
wind and rain.
Long beak
sword-like
and lightning lit.

It was the biggest
Motherfucking
heron I'd ever seen.

You cringe
at my choice of words,
but I was confronted
with Storm God Zeus
grown bored
with his Swan disguise,
and I wouldn't
leave any
lady folk
alone with him.

Burning

The propane burner roars
weeds and dry grass
burst into flame
hot ash buries itself in my hair
I will smell of smoke
for days.

My job allows little time
for weeding
Delicacy is not an option
Once a month
I scour the gravel strewn lot
with gouts of cleansing flame

Fireworks often leave me indifferent
but watching acres of weeds
suddenly combust
and to know
that I am the cause
fills me with a modest joy.

I set upon
one last patch of dandelions
green with golden manes
and filled with life
Scorned and despised weeds
they retain a beauty of their own
My torch turns them
to orange embers & black ash
within seconds
It teaches me
most beauty will go
unrecognized, and
all beauty
must die.

Killdeer Blues

Silver-grey dawn
Pacific Northwest
Hung-over
Gravel crunches under foot
as I approach my car.
The sound begins again.
Plaintive yet piercing
a tiny heart rent asunder.

I turn to
spastic flutter of feathers
rich brown, striped with black and white.
One wing extended awkwardly
the other clutched tight.
The entire tiny mass
turns eccentric circles.

"Give up the game, Mama bird.
I'm sick of this shit!"
The avian ruse continues
Thespian mama feigns injury
hoping to draw me
away from her eggs.

As the bird cry assaults my skull
I wonder why
I keep helping
the thankless wretches.
Surely the future sight
of puffballs on stilts
skittering across my lot
is not enough.

Ground nesting dullards
gravel loving halfwits

126

I erect sawhorses and yellow tape
to keep two dozen RV owners
from killing them.
On mornings like these
I ponder
whether evolution would be served
by letting them die.

Antediluvian

New feet on new earth
free willed but rule bound
happy in the fat of the land
but discontent

An early appearance
by the imp of the perverse
gives birth to an idea:
"The path of excess leads to wisdom"

Graceless gourmandry from fruit
to fungi to flowering poppies
Touting new perceptions
that are naught
but broken distortions of the old.

Falling carelessly into flesh pits
casting aside known loves
for new flavors
carefully consensual
but supremely selfish.

The world grown old and tired
simple pleasures seldom seen.
The first large drops
of holy water rain
presage the coming deluge.

Springtime is Hard on the Little Things

Early morning commute
favoring the farmland
rather than the interstate
possum
possum
possum
possum
crow crouched on kitten's corpse.

The gravel grumbles under my wheels
as I pull into my parking spot.
Yellow warning tape flutters
above knocked over saw horses.
Apparently my warnings
failed to protect
the ground nested eggs
from the errant driving
of RV owning idiots.
The killdeer parents
screamed and keened
as I ambled over to my work shed.

Today was to be about the back acreage,
overgrown and wild.
The mower's mulching blades
were replaced for ones with higher lift
and its blower was opened wide.
Rolling the machine towards
the rampant greenery,
I pause before starting,
memories of last year's massacre
make me ill with images
of mower mangled
bunny bits.

Never again,
I promise myself
and any unseen mini mammals.
I noisily scuffle and scour
every inch of weed riddled greenery.
I seem to succeed in scaring away
dozens of baby bunnies.
Fur balls smaller than my clenched fist
run riot in random directions
until
satisfied I return to man my machine.

Freshly sharpened blades
makes short work
of grass, dandelion and thistle.
Some scampering catches my eye
and I spot a pair of little lepus
attempting to leap up
the back of the building.
Laughingly, I scold them
for not heading into neighboring fields,
and as I promise
that they are safe enough
where they are
I hear a disheartening crunch
from beneath the blades.

Unrecognizable bits
of bone, fur and gristle
shoot suddenly from the blower.
I cut the engine
and examine the fleshy pile
of a bunny
that froze instead of fled
when I tromped across the field
earlier.

My heart sinks a little,
and I'm oddly angry
at the wee beastie

for not having the sense
to flee
at my provocation.
No time for nonsense
I return to my duty
and mow
for almost an hour
without incident.

Mere feet from the finish
I suddenly stop
for reasons I can't quite fathom.
Unthinking, I kneel
and discover another
fear frozen critter
inches from the wheel.
I cradle him in my cupped hand,
look him closely in the eye
and lecture him on safety
while escorting him to the edge
of my yard.

Just beyond the fence
an evil looking ram
bleats disgust at my foolishness.

Funeral March of the Raccoons

Dan was the best of us.
More altruistic, calm and competent.,
less drinking, no drugs,
healthier and happier
He biked from Seattle to Portland yearly.
He had adopted an orphaned Chinese girl.
Whatever fates had kept our debauched selves alive,
had determined to take Dan.

Esophageal cancer
Spread into bones and brain.
A quiet battle everyday
and all victories Pyrrhic.
Two years were gained
longer than experts imagined.

Routine, ever the bane of emotion,
raised its featureless head
and gazed upon us all.
Every new medical complication
meant a new round of visitation
for who knew when the end would come?

I arrived sans hope or fear,
a stop in passing,
en route to holiday.
The mood more somber than ever,
I entered the bedroom,
and Dan lay contorted
a beardless Christ
in a secular Pieta.
I moved to grasp a gnarled hand,
when a sour wind passed over gravel
and through his lips.

Privileged to have witnessed his passing,
I paused for hours,
hoping to be of service to his wife and family.
Sadly superfluous, I left
and stood on the lawn without purpose.
Wishing I could weep,
I called my mom
and babbled moronically,
while unconsciously watching
four raccoons
try to cross
the raging arterial.

Their leader seemed wise to the ways of traffic
pausing then sprinting where appropriate.
Almost across,
a truck came barreling around the corner.
Four fur balls ran and rolled
ending disheveled and disheartened
but unharmed
in a heap at my feet.

My talk ceased as I stared agog
at their fuzzy forms.
After a dazed moment
the leader barked
and they rose to quickly circle me.
Tiny arms raised over their heads,
the four figures walked clockwise
looking like wee Greek dancers.

Another bark
and they were gone.
Leaving me
to ponder mysteries
both great and small.

Auction Day

The warehouse cat scratches my shoulder
scrambling to retain his perch
as the hundreds of bidders arrive.
The auctioneer mainlines coffee
and winks at me as the proceedings begin

Pee stained mattress
Two boxes of old paperbacks.

The first unit is small and almost empty when opened.
Quiet and courteous Kristen was the renter.
She started college in the east,
moved away from her folks for the first time,
and filled the unit with personal trinkets
too impractical to take with her.
A year in she broke down and dropped out,
payment stopped and now everything has passed
to the toothless junk dealer
who bid twenty dollars.

Professional weight set
Stacks of family photos

Manny Palau was a big boy
a 'roid raging gym rat,
impending divorce made him gather his gear here.
Around town he would buy me beer
and gab guiltily about family fights.
Soon he was in the slammer for assault
and Manny's mom paid for storage until she passed.
Now a scrawny red neck wrangles weights
purchased for one hundred fifty.

Antique roll-top desk
Crazy colored steamer trunk

Twenty years together, yet Robin and Ray never married.
The palimony case complicated issues of ownership.
A lifetime left stored and farming dust,
one would pay and then the other
until uncertainty of who would prevail
prevented either from caring for the property.
Professionals now take possession
as the antique store truck pulls into position.

Oils from local artists
Several sizable pieces of statuary

Gray haired Gary was gay
but waited to reveal it until his son was grown.
The wife didn't take it well
and Gary's treasures were set aside
while he hunted for the perfect pad.
I found it funny and flattering when he hit on me,
whoever killed him hadn't.
Unusual art dealers battle and bid
I won't watch to see who wins.

World War Two bayonet
Ancient Indian katar

Lorne wrote letters
I never had a chance to meet him.
Alone and in his eighties,
he stashed piles of precious personals,
and retired to Alaska
long before I became employed here.
One day the letters stopped
and now I have to hear howls of joy
as ecstatic assholes
preen over newly purchased prizes.

The auctioneer hands me stacks of cash,
a remarkable boon to the business.
Yet, as I watch the winning bidders,

I see only vermin and vultures,
uncaring pests and parasites.
My stomach roils with sympathy
for the unloved and the unlucky,
the sorrowful and the psychotic,
and I wish I could return
what once was theirs.

Gomita De Tamarindo Con Chile

Proud to be a redneck,
although he prefers the term mesh back
'cuz he's country but he ain't Southern,
He swaggers big and bear-like
from the pickup with the "git 'er done" bumper sticker.
A baseball bat rolls in the back,
blood spattered from rousting illegals.

As he enters the corner store,
 a steadfast anger reawakens.
How could an American store be filled
with so many items in Spanish?
But no outward sign of his anger is visible,
after all he's here to buy Mexican candy.

He can't remember why he had tried them,
jellied tamarind pieces covered in powdered chili.
The very presence of such strange food
was evidence of the trespassers in his valley.
Yet after trying them, he craved them weekly.

The musky, sweet flavor of the tamarind
reminded him of the taste of his girl as she came.
The powdered chili bit him back after each swallow.
He took this as the price to be paid for his desire,
a fiery foreign flavor fighting his advances.

The Argument Has Long Been Over

He quotes Thoreau at me,
my mad mirror image
and dour doppelganger.

Drowning in the stink of my own sweat,
I scowl at his words
and load the last crate onto the truck.
"Self-reliant, my ass!
That wordsmith was a grubber of coins
from friends and family."

He jerks skyward and self important.
" . . . but in the eyes of posterity,
which means more,
the words of wisdom,
or base biography?"

I sigh and slam the gate shut,
sending the truck on its way.
Neck crack and shoulder roll,
there's no need to answer.
He could only ever have one reply
nestled as he is
upon my weary back
at the base of my tired brain.

The Tedious Responsibilities of the Protagonist

. . . could've danced
with the buxom girl
of Russian winter eyes,
but he doesn't dance
anymore than Steve McQueen
would drive a Prius.

Real world worries
are beyond his grasp.
Frightened of paper tigers,
he pulls on the tails of dragons
the better to kick them
in the nuts.

The whimsy of cloud hopping heroines
has been ground up
in the gears of the god machine
and audience expectation
has him there
ready to make them a sandwich
after they fall.

Aristotle's ghost
yelled at me
to start this piece
in medias res.
I'm not sure I give a shit,
but I did it anyway,
and the protagonist doesn't seem to mind,
He knows it's all in the telling.

Laurels Given and Taken Away

The black moods have come again,
agony of acid and stone
roiling and rolling in my guts.
The accusations of ancestors
condemning my lack of ambition
echo in my mind.

Present employment is ending,
and the future seems
comprised more of compromise
than paths of glory.
No job yet has been
what I've studied for
or dreamed of.
The best of them
were life support systems
for artistic dreams,
they provided only
a hardscrabble existence
but at least
I lived happy.

. . . but today,
today I live in uncertainty
as I roll,
iron willed and duty bound,
into my volunteer work.

We gather in the basement
of the non-profit art house cinema,
here to plan a festival of film noir
for the upcoming season.
The sponsors are here,
local businessmen
with a noir favorite or two
eager to discover old films
of similar ilk.

The projectionist is present
laid back and knowledgeable,
primarily concerned with availability
of the films chosen.
I was asked to attend
and welcomed warmly
for my expertise,
my film freakdom and wit.
Last to arrive
an odd woman
younger than I,
but with the demeanor
of a depression era schoolmarm,
from the volunteer pool
she was simply eager
to see her opinions
have a concrete effect
on something,
anything.

Films are proposed,
and when asked
I opine on the picture's place
in film history,
its innovations,
and its potential appeal
to our temperamental audience.
After my own proposals,
the schoolmarm sniffs,
"Never heard of 'em"
cracks open her copy
of a Leonard Maltin guide
and lists films she thinks
sound interesting.

The vote goes smoothly,
the genre is well represented
and I prepared to return
to my rotten mood
when. . .

the sponsors speak up,
and propose
I lead a lecture series
ten minutes
before and after each film
to tell a brief history of the pic
and amusing anecdotes about
actors of old.

Something tickles,
a puff of pride perhaps?
A creeping bit of self-esteem
raises its head
from the trenches
of employment woes,
and as words of acceptance and thanks
tremble on the edge of my lips,
the schoolmarm interjects,
"Why him?
We're all volunteers,
I'd like to lecture."
When asked
what she knows about film
she simply snorts,
"I do my homework!"

Everything seems awkward
and no one wants to argue
so without a vote
and no understanding
of how it's come to this,
the schoolmarm is given
equal time before the audience.

My belly growls
and my brain grumbles
as I watch her pack her books
to leave the conference room.
She grinds her teeth,
and her eyes flare

as if we'd spited her.
I sigh dispiritedly
suspecting that
whatever she gets from this
is more
than I need,
and I return home
to rewrite my resume.

Sons of Death

"Civilized men are more discourteous than savages because they know they can
be impolite without having their skulls split, as a general thing."
--Robert E Howard

The urge to spit in society's eye
is instinctual in men
a Freudian attempt to usurp the Father's place
and enact their own law.

Some Celtic tribes saw the good
in this rebellion
and allowed their fractious youth
to do whatever they pleased
as Sons of Death
but free of society's rules
meant free of society's protection
and anyone could do anything
to a Son of Death
without fear
of repercussion.
In time, the survivors
would always return to the fold
of civilization's embrace.

I've done my time as a Son of Death
Tested parents and friends, teachers and cops,
Seen how far I could take an insult
in a bar full of strangers
Seduced a married woman
just to see if I could
and while the consequences were never pleasant
I treasure the broken bones,
the shame-faced mornings after
the final sense of doing myself a wrong
by doing wrong to others

I scarcely see
today's Sons of Death
I hear echoes of half-hearted actions
false identities on the internet
mocking screeds in a digital medium
out of society when online
but of it when off
There's no challenge in that
no sense of self versus society
safely protected while spitting venom
Why return to the fold
when they're already under shelter.
If only I could show them
the value of
a good ass-kicking.

The Coming Storm

It smells of ozone and cow shit here,
hog killin' humid but it ain't hot,
the grass slithers greedily over itself
eager for the heavens' piss.

The boss man berates me,
casting aspersions on my abilities.
Don't have much to say to that,
this is not what I was trained for,
this is not where I'm meant to be.

An abscessed tooth throbs deep in my head,
spreading rot throughout my thoughts.
There's no insurance here,
the VA won't see me for weeks
and the free clinic's got me pegged
as a pill grubbin' problem patient.

Pounding fence posts
is no way to earn your daily bread.
My sore muscles spasm
as the first lightning bolt strikes,
the sledge slips sideways
splintering the edge of the post
before thudding to the ground.

From behind me,
a curse is called out with my name in it.
I heft my hammer and wonder . . .
. . . just how much damage I could do with it
before the storm abates.

Drinking With the Hunted

It happens on many a dog growl night,
the blue-collar bohemians
swagger with their half-assed Hemingway shtick
and descend upon the bars
notebooks in hand
pretending to be Bukowski.

I liked them no more
than the critics
the academics
or Bukowski himself did,
but I was there too,
finding love with dogs from hell,
playing the piano with bleeding fingers
and drowning in the ordinary madness.

The imitators irritate,
and the so-called scholars
who dismiss him
seem lacking in life experience.
That old drunk makes me want to write
like no one else can.

He wrote,
I write,
and this poem is for him.

Avec Moi le Deluge

Fridays from happy hour to close,
he sits rooted to the end of the bar,
a slab of granite pushed above ground
by a fit of tectonic distemper.

To be in his presence
is to sense a world of calluses and scars,
a y-chromosome aura drifts in the pleasant musk
of hard won sweat created from heavy labor.

Instantly recognizable to all the regulars,
no one knew him beyond banal pleasantries,
merely another monosyllabic mutterer
in an ocean of sports speculation and weather witticisms.

Almost beneath notice a single tear escaped his eye
one clear, cold Friday evening.
A barmaid glimpsed it falling
as she scooped his tip into her apron,
but the tear was fleeting
and she was too busy to give it any thought.

A week passed by and a hard breeze blew
the bar doors open wide.
When they shut again, he'd walked in
and it was obvious he'd been crying.
Had his woman left or dog just died?
No one knew enough to say,
and silently shamed by masculine tears
no one drew close to ask.

On Friday next, the town grew dark
as thunderheads rolled in.
The jukebox bumped Thorogood off
as lightning lit up the streets,
and before the end of the thunder roll
he had sat in his seat again.

Two tear torn trails led down his cheeks
and they made the rain look weak.
Fellow patrons whispered not a word
but slowly exited as they saw him.
The staff trembled as they served his typical orders
and couldn't wait to call it a night.

A week of solid, driving rain
made the river jump the revetment.
The bar was closed that Friday
and the sandbags failed to save it.
A near endless whirl of sports souvenirs
and bud light bottles
poured out of the gutted tavern,
the only business in town
to suffer significantly.

A surprising Saturday sun
beat down upon the wreckage
and a bloated body on the shore.
The cops will never ID it,
but the owners, bartenders, servers and patrons
of the nearby bar all know him better
than they could put into words.

Killers

Sometimes I still taste the blood,
that skinhead's life
roiling around in my mouth.
In dreams I still watch
the date rapist tumble
over the balcony
from my well timed shove.
Had those fights gone further
would I now be a killer?
****

I.
CPS was a b-boy
crip walkin', fast talkin',
his Dr. J natural
bobbed above his dome
as he headed, hat in hand,
into the interview.

He feared his felonies
would prevent his employment.
We talked.
I wasn't worried.
The puckered bullet scar on his face
crinkled close as he smiled
when I hired him.

I lived across the street from the projects.
CPS and I walked to work together
regularly.
We always left early and never lagged,
because cops would stop us
regularly,
knowing nothing good could come
from a hirsute white boy
hanging
with a crip walkin' ex-banger.

150

Casual conversation on the commute
often turned
to the craft of crack-slinging
on the hot Houston streets,
anecdotes about Uzi notes
ringing wrathful
against shotgun shacks.
Murder always reduced to manslaughter
as long as
killers only killed killers.

Sometime after CPS described his search
for the straight and narrow,
the bullet that bounced off
his chiseled cheekbone,
and his sidestep to Seattle
where no one knew his name,
I realized
that despite his skill as a storyteller
I could never picture
his finger on the trigger
and all that parole board paperwork
seemed no more
than bureaucratic bullshit.

II.
In the drunken days
of dorm room debauch,
many a bash ended
to the sound
of bellicose bellowing.
A thirty-something
crazed Columbian
berating college coeds
in broken English.

Hugo's dad made mad money,
so Hugo lived the life
of a perpetual exchange student.

In Germany and Japan,
Georgia Tech and Evergreen State,
he enrolled and matriculated
but seldom attended classes
preferring to perfect the pursuit
of the fairer sex.

He found my little liberal arts college
to be fully frustrating
filled with feminists and lesbians
who wouldn't look twice at him.
The men seemed to all be maricones,
smiling simps and willing weaklings
craving scraps from this world of women.

I met him while policing a party,
asked to escort him away
from some understandably fearful females.
Squinty eyed and machete marked,
he boasted I wasn't bad enough
to make him move.
There were words and wrestling,
a few fists were flung,
until he stumbled down the stairs
and into the night.
Days later he brought me booze,
and declared
I was the only one around
man enough to drink with him.

Never admitting his loneliness
or understanding why people avoided him,
he made me his fast friend.
We drank and drugged,
and he would attempt
to win and woo my friends
through liberal usage
of his vast stacks of cash.

He bought us
cheap cars and expensive electronics,
and the parties were forever and always
on him.

We went shooting once,
smoking Cuban cigars
and firing AK's
at an out of the way range
in redneck Ville.
A fifth of tequila in,
accuracy wavered
and Hugo spun tales
of hunting humans.
Jeep jaunts into the jungle
spraying lead
at bow wielding indios.
He grinned as we stood aghast
and we left
deciding he must be joking.

Months passed
and Hugo had returned
to his pursuit of sex
in foreign lands
and I thought of him only
as a source
of amusing anecdote,
until . . .
my routine was ruined
by FBI agents
needing to talk to me.
They arrived
photos in hand
of me
arm in assault weapon carrying arm
with the son
of a notorious drug lord.

They wanted to know
all I could tell them
about Hugo.
It wasn't much
and it came out hard,
because my thoughts were tangled
with the image
of my darkly grinning drinking buddy
gutting indians
outside the emerald mines
deep into the interior of Columbia.

III.
The towers fell
and Michael enlisted,
against the advice
of parents and pals.
He was gung-ho and gone
to Afghanistan
before we could blink.

A scant couple of years later
and his hands shook at dinner
as he told us a tale:

Security detail
escorting an unfamiliar officer
as he questioned
a number of informants.

Taliban Terry the turncoat,
a cartoonishly nicknamed
mutt of a man
sold stories and invented info
for any American who asked.
He bent over backwards
bare-necked and unctuous

when Michael's unit
perused his place.

The officer talked with Terry,
hands were clapped
wives were summoned to serve.
Five twelve year old girls,
the bent-backed betrothed of Terry,
walked about the property
offering water to soldiers
under orders to ignore them.

A burqa clad, frail form
wobbles
and wordlessly falls into the dust.

There are shouts
and a corpsman is summoned
against Terry's fervent protests.
Clothes are cut
a fetid stench rises
gagging those gathered round.
Pus and rot dominate
the area under the girl's tiny waist.
A deep set infection had set in,
the result of genitals sewn shut
to prevent possible predation
from American soldiers.

Events moved faster
than Michael could recall in detail.
The officer gave many orders
through thin lips stretched taut.
The girl and other wives were whisked away
and Terry shouted and postured petulantly.
As the officer left,
he mentioned to the men
that Terry had no more information to provide.

Michael stared down the dinner table
and paused
before telling us what it felt like
to kick a man to death.
I watched as he left the table,
the shape of a man
I knew to be kind hearted,
and I wondered
if his soul would ever
stop bleeding.

****

Sometimes I still see the blood spurt
from the fractured skull
of my girlfriend's stalker.
Late night I wonder
how close I've come
to killing a man,
and the boundary seems vast
inconceivable,
until I realize
that I have friends who've crossed it.
This thought silences me
and I can only weep for them.

Tired of Talking

Some sorry word salad
is life.

Noted and notable writer
unable to express even
one day's dilemma
without revealing
his own hypocrisies.

Wanting to write
"woe is me."
while wailing
at the echoing tide,
fully aware
he lives lovingly
without boundaries
while both the sheep
and the shackled
surround him.

Soup kitchen service
and fence post pounding
push ego and id
into comfortable
quietude.
At least until
the forces of night
leap the hedges
to ask,
"Are You a Good Person?"

. . . and every drop of blood
and ink that spill
try to answer that question.

I Want to Enter My House Justified

Mind ablaze with debt dread
and the friction of love buried
under worldly pressures,
I suffer insomnia
and drown in the wet cotton reality
of deep cable programming
in the hours before dawn.

Swaddled in sweat clothes,
big toe jutting from an ever growing hole
in an army surplus tube sock,
I grasp the remote control
as if it were the cliff grown wild strawberry
from the oft quoted zen koan.

This glass teat
this electronic narcotic
feeds me
washes over me
numbs me
allows a life of cowardice
and craven compromise
to become bearable
while a world of opportunity
passes out of reach.

Suddenly I wake
(though I'd never been asleep)
confronted by family.
My grandfather's cousin,
the old cowboy actor,
strides tall and proud
through the dust
of an old Peckinpah pic.
Alert, I watch
and watching, learn.

"I want to enter my house justified",
answers the world weary Joel McCrea
as he lays dying in the final reel.
No slave to robber barons
and the minions of Mammon
who grind men's souls for profit,
nor reckless rebel
bloodying the innocent
to shake the status quo,
he took a third path
and found it fatal.

He died not for what he believed in,
but because he refused to accept
the options offered to him
were the only ones available.

From near my undisturbed bed
the alarm sounds
as the credits roll,
and aided by a bit of celluloid morality
I don my spurs and hat
and head out to the workaday world
hoping to return home
justified.

Just One Sin

In my family,
solidly Scots Presbyter,
the only sin worth mentioning
was Sloth.
Steal something,
and the only question
was how you would pay it back.
Knock a girl up,
how would you support the kid?
Blacken an eye or break a nose,
how much labor would be lost
for you or your victim?

Work hard enough
and anything can be forgiven,
slack and be irreversibly lost.

 In all a rather practical religion,
but still vexing in its own way.
The hierarchy of blessed work
every bit as complicated
as keeping track of saints.
Food, shelter, and clothing
provide these and be exalted.
Caregivers, doctors and nurses
are begrudgingly given blessings
of their own.
It all goes downhill after that,
until nestled just above
beggars,
artists and entertainers are found.

There's no doubt I'm one of the damned,
but like a lapsed Catholic
still feeling guilty
for gawking at flesh revealed,

I find myself
contemptuous
of other artists
who don't sweat
when working their day job.

As I put pen to paper,
lounging in the grass
on a summer afternoon,
I feel a Presbyterian devil
at my side.
Not half as entertaining
as the imps sent to tempt
Catholics,
he merely busies himself
prodding the clouds
into interesting shapes
to distract me,
knowing I'll fall for it
every time.

Sure Lock Holmes

Smoking stogies in the sun,
pausing between plays
at the Ashland
Shakespeare festival
I find flyers
of gorgeous goldenrod
nestled among the trees.

SURE LOCK HOLMES
No crime too small to solve
A solid track record
of recovering stolen bikes,
uncovering toilet paper vandals,
and discovering new uses
for old stories.

Reasonable rates.
Discount for Ashland HS
student body members.

A pair of giggling girls
are pictured within
those words.
One wearing a deerstalker
and holding a magnifying glass
up to her baby blues,
the other simply strokes
a walrus like moustache
above her gamine grin.

My afternoon time warped,
watching Scooby-Doo
amidst the plastic toy detritus
of a five year old's summer Saturday,
reading Encyclopedia Brown
during my eighth winter

cocooned in blankets
sure I could solve any crime
given enough time
and an answer key
at the back of a book,
a fourteen year old grumbling
at a mother forever watching
Agatha Christie
too cool to admit
that I always had to find out
who done it.

Later,
as I lounged about the deck
of a riverside pub
I decided to interview
these clever cuties,
perhaps produce an article
for a local rag.

They answered the phone
simultaneously,
not sisters but nearly inseparable.
I was cheerfully charmed.
Fierce at fifteen,
they were disappointed
at their inability
to find employment of merit,
so half in fun
but hoping for cash
they turned to
low rent sleuthing.

They told me tall tales
in a lavish language
conjoining Conan Doyle
with west coast teen idiom:
The Case of the Scarlet Skateboard,
The Mystery on Mount Ashland,
and the Riddle of the Slow Scooter.

163

Three calls of three hours each,
and they always left me laughing,
energized and feeling half my age.

I occasionally come across the article
amidst my piles of papers,
never finished and thus never sold.
I've tried to tell friends and family
about my encounter
with these inventive ingénues,
but they either roll their eyes
or suggest something sordid
about my intentions.
I'm deeply disappointed
that they can't see
the sweet and simple sentiment
the girls awoke in me
and how grand and glorious
their lives are sure to be.

Gone Feral

In love with the world,
but I bite.
Sans fear or anger
the outstretched hand
still gets the fang.

The gray-muzzled hound
left behind
at the summer cabin.
Who is to say what I've seen
between abandonment
and family's return.

Surplus kitten
never knowing
food without forage.
Are you seeking
companionship
without domestication?

We can fend for each other,
easier than for ourselves
and the leash
or the collar
need never come into it.

She Fears My Praise

The door is wide open,
as she waits
for me to take her to dinner.
I enter with a smile for the dog,
and ardent words of praise
for her.
She giggles, kisses me
then scolds me
saying that my words
are too much,
too soon.

I attempt to massage her feet,
but she is far too ticklish
so we cuddle instead.
Too distracted by her eyes
to watch TV
I nibble on her ear
and whisper
She pulls away
slightly,
smiles and says,
"You can't know that!"

Awash in the afterglow
my brain is heady with scent and sex
my fingers play about her body
as she sighs, long, languorous
and content.
A burst of verbal affection
escapes my lips.
She throws a leg
over mine
and replies,
"You can't say that.
You'll only be disappointed
later."

Bolt upright
with the alarm.
I must rush
to get to work
I lower my lips
to her cheek,
as she snuggles into her pillow
and finally
I can speak my adoration
as she deserves.

Our Own Eden

I awoke beside you
to discover the gates wide open.
No angel with flaming sword
to deny us entry.

Hand in hand
we strode freely
past Elysium and Arcadia
and entered the garden
designed for us.

The world's been named
all work accomplished,
there's nothing for us to do
save enter the bower
as Milton described
and glory in each other's flesh
with a hard won
and new found
innocence.

Freed from prior punishment
the serpent walks the garden anew,
but his temptations are old,
familiar,
and oddly laughable.
Yet,
you should know,
I'll gladly eat
any fruit you proffer,
and happily take
any blame
upon myself
entirely.

Romance and Loss

Megan's man proposed to her
the day her mama died.
She gasped, delighted, at the ring
then crumpled as she cried.

A fatal fall down icy stairs
had been her mother's fate.
Megan had just got off the phone
when Chad showed for their date.

The date cut short, her head a whirl,
Megan sobbed in bed for hours.
Chad lingered in the living room
alone with sagging flowers.

Her family scrapbook caught his eye
and Chad looked beneath the cover.
Photo and story jumped out at him
and he planned to cheer his lover.

One week later he proposed again
in a forest by a stream.
A faint memory tugged at her,
she let out a gentle scream.

He'd reenacted every move
Megan's dad gave to her mom,
in scene, in setting, in tender kiss
and the reading of a psalm.

Megan had hoped that Chad would be
the beau her mom would bless,
and now with spirit watching up above
she knew she could say yes.

No Lessons to be Learned

She lay uneasy on love tossed sheets
tracing the white web of scars
upon her lover's inner arm.

"They're not important,"
was his answer
to queries about their cause.

She didn't press or prod,
figuring he would tell in time,
but time has come and gone again
and no answer has arrived.

It would not trouble her half so much,
if he were a secretive sort,
but his heart's as open
as the wide, blue sea
and he's shown his soul to her.

She always listens
to his tall tales,
and he revels in the telling.
She glimpses truth
when he talks of sex,
both shameful and transcendent.
She hears his hurt
when he talks of wars
both righteous and inane
But for all his talk
and deep confessions
his scars remain unnamed.

One wine filled night
she crawls to him,
a razor in her hand,
convinced she'll find
the source of the scars

if she could only view them
from within.

"Don't do that again."
he says,
with love and laughter
in his eyes.
The razor passes from her
and they dally upon the bed.

Until . . .

She lay uneasy on love tossed sheets
tracing the white web of scars
upon her lover's inner arm.

Green-Eyed Creatures

The Cat:

More aggressively affectionate
with each evening I'm absent,
nosing the overnight bag each morning
neutered but knowing
the nature of the new scents
he considers making his mark
but glides away at my sharp word

The Dog:

A new friend, new toys, more walks
her pup praises my presence
couch ejected, but not dejected
open mouthed joy at human company
until in horror exiled from the bedroom
he crouches in a corner
trying to lick holes in his fur

Butterball and I

I.
"C'mon, Dummy,"
I say in my best Fred Sanford imitation.

Merry and awkward
the fur ball trundles toward the door.
Stubby Lhasa Apso legs
carry the plump poodle torso.
He gazes up at me while I fasten the leash,
all bulging eyes and protruding teeth.
I've known him less than a year
yet I'm already tired
of the so ugly he's cute description,
however apt it may be.

He's my girlfriend's dog,
but I promise him
that I would never deny ownership,
I wouldn't want to slight the little mutant.
He ignores me as he moves toward the car,
rolling forward as if each of his four legs
were a different length.

I babble at the wee beast
as we drive to the park.
He ignores me,
too excited by the prospect
of new adventure,
and I'm reminded
that the rescued dog
had once been perpetually housebound.

The pooch practically explodes
when confronted with
the opportunities the park presents.
He strains at the leash
seeking to go all directions at once.

In short order
he shits
seven times
in seven different places
in as many minutes.

Finally freed of earthly affairs
he floats us toward
the leash free
portion of the park.

II.
Butterball seeks canine society
and this Sunday morning
the park is filled with his brethren.

I leave the leash on
cautious about B B's lack
of social skills,
but the new pup at the park
is warmly welcomed
by mammals of many stripes.
He butts heads
with a Bisson Friche
while his new friend's
elderly Asian owner
attempts to stuff
him full of homemade treats.

Black labs and boxers,
golden retrievers,
and a passel
of pint-sized critters
with French monikers
all sniff and skitter
in playful abandon.
Butterball joins in,
but behaves himself,

looking perpetually perplexed
that the world
could be this wonderful.

Eventually,
the doggy domination games
become a bit much,
and I have to extract my pal
from a canine
group grope.

III.
We settle on a saunter
around the park's periphery,
encountering dogs and owners
one on one
seemed more our speed.
I had half-forgotten
how humans have
their own forms
of ass-sniffing
domination games.

We passed a garrulous gal
and her watchful Rottweiler.
They soaked in the spectacle
of the odd little dog leading
my leather jacket clad,
beringed and cigar smoking self.
She suddenly spoke up,
"What's with all the manly macho shit?
Are you compensating for
walking a girly dog?"
"Sorry sister," I replied,
"Your analysis is unwarranted
and unwelcome.
Sometimes a guy
just likes to smoke a good cigar."

We turned across
an old horseshoe pitch
and were casually accosted
by a teen in a trucker cap.
He blinked twice at Butterball
and asked if I were gay.
"Sorry son,
I don't swing that way,
but I'm sure you'll find
a boyfriend someday."
He silently summed up
the bullying math,
and decided against
any unfortunate action.

Short stubby legs slowed down
a pace or two,
so we started back.
A comely co-ed,
complete with ponytail
and running gear,
stopped short
at the sight of Butterball.
"Either you're walking
your girlfriend's dog,
or you're here to pick up girls,"
she stated with certainty.
"He belongs to my girlfriend"
"That's a shame," she said smiling
and resumed her running.
I paused ,
uncertain how to take
the apparent compliment.

In the car, I apologized
to Butterball for breaking my promise.
"I'm sorry I didn't acknowledge you,
Buddy,
but you understand
how these territorial pissings work,

she was sniffing out my lines and limits,
and it wouldn't do
for her to spread her scent
in my yard."
Butterball yawned,
and waited to get back home
to mom.

Looking at a Dead Dog

Nightly news anchors
report on the search
for hikers
missing since the recent floods,
my nerves jangle
as they spend more time
talking
and calculating
the cost of the search
over identifying
with the fate of the lost.

A neo-con knucklehead opines
that public funds
should not be spent so,
and even my level headed lady
suggests
people should not spend time
in woods deep and mountains high
for mere recreation.

I once had a neighbor
who never
took his dog for a walk.
Wiggling and playful
the black lab
would run ruinous laps
around a yard
containing only dirt.

The digging began suddenly
as much with mouth
as with paw,
a feverish attempt
at communing
with the Earth
source of all life.

The digging ended suddenly
the old girl keeled over dead,
her immense belly
distended with dirt.
Her owner and I
(from across the fence)
watched solemnly
as her death rattle
produced a vomiting
of blood flecked mud.

The Sioux have a saying,
only the very good
or the very evil
may look upon a dead dog
directly.

It's Going to Be Okay

His hands sweat
on first dates
or holding a gun

but that's okay, because

She's awkwardly aroused
by angry male voices
and animated explosions

Moving in means examining
the detritus of each other's past

She lives lightly
a cigarette case,
a Czech glass vase
mementos of joyful moments
from every relationship
good or bad

He rolls heavy
warehousing boxes of books
crates of arrowheads,
archeological debris
A careful chronicle of the individual
with only the pain excised

It's all going to be okay
as long as she does the decorating.

Justice is a Commodity

Jesus hangs around her neck,
the crucifix askew,
thin gold chain accentuating
the purple and blue
bruises.
The emerald green
of weed and reed
conceals
the grey brown muck
her corpse sinks into
under the overpass.

The delinquent daughter
of a friend
of my girl,
I gather drips and drabs
of the tattered tale
of her untimely demise.

My misspent imagination
conjures a geriatric jogger
discovering the body
as I drive by a nearby
bike shop
on my morning commute.

More musings on the murder
picture a carnal embrace
grown vicious and violent
while my sweetie and I
were watching Fifties film noir
snuggling on the sofa.

The word came down,
drugs had been found
and the virtue of our victim
had been smudged.

The DA declared the case closed.
The possible drug death
of a chick with a runaway rep
and a rap sheet longer than most
allowed cops to neglect
the blood and the bruising
on the body
found under the overpass.

Work weary
and day job drained
I follow my sweetie
to a blue collar bar,
where the rowdy and raucous
are raffling off prizes.

I query the cause
of this furious fundraising.
"An autopsy," they answer
"for the forsaken,
but not friendless,
girl who died
under the overpass."

Cash is collected
and a check deposited
into the arguably affluent
account of the coroner.
The old man does his duty,
and with the quiet clatter
of scalpel and saw
proves the bad bruises
on the slender throat
mean the girl on the gurney
was strangled.

Cops come around
and ask the obvious questions
to friends, family and the odd
potential witness.

A single suspect soon arises
from amongst the mass:
a stranger to the city
and the man last seen
with the victim.

Cops call other cops,
a digital ear is put to the wind,
and the man is traced to another town.
DNA evidence proves positively
his hands were on her throat.

The news wends its way around,
and the blue collar bar
shouts in collective triumph,
as a distraught mom
graces the detectives with gratitude.
Somewhere outside the social circle
I grumble to myself
about civil servants
who only perform their jobs
when the costs are covered
by someone else.

There's no counting
the number of corpses,
lying in the muck and mud
covered by the emerald green
of weed and reed,
who will never know justice
as there is no one
to pay for the autopsy.

New Fire in Winter

To seize, to conquer,
I know that dream.
My ardor shall never sleep
My eyes never forget.
Even half-dead, there'll be no time for secrets.
I cast aside the prophet of what's to be,
just an echo in a coal mine,
trying to bind God with words.
A verbal tomb,
and linguistic prison
grasping for pure consciousness.
Somewhere, past the timber line,
bears cower at my thunder.
I would hold high converse
where the winds gather,
and leap over the assumptions
of young artists
tripping over their shoelaces.
One day I shall remember
the chaff burning away,
vault doors swinging open,
the sight of myself at play.
I had gone to sea with a sigh
in a boat drained of the sublime.
The Good day has yet to arrive:
my own house, with a high pine,
deep shade, and birds.
I listen close
for growing wind down narrow alleys,
desperate construction during the cruelest months,
and the fresh spark of new fires.
I'm the guardian of winter weeds
growing year round in the garden.
The stone walks, where are they?
I've yet to clear them of ice.
I deny the soil it's fallow time.

I've never been made of sweetness and light
only now have I discovered self-delight.
Crawling atop the rock,
my hair between me and the sun,
the waves ripple out from me.
My feet aren't done with the earth,
rich loam emboldens me.
I was careless in my growing,
but I'll not regret
my twisted stalks.

If I were a young man,
I would tremble at knowing
the fine rage of my current age.

The shadows are full, endlessly internal.
I follow the purposeful wind
to the house and the pasture beyond.
The cindery snow melts before my touch
Ashes to me, and dust to me,
I question Death's inevitability.
The recurring inane and helplessly absurd
are my only obstacles.
I care deeply about crossroads
and collect old sheaves of paper.
I hear, more and more,
my own distinct voice.
In the cold air,
my spirit
awakens.

About the Author

photo by Marika Garland of Photography by Marika

Neil McCrea is a poet and author living in the Pacific Northwest. His work has most recently appeared in *Knock, Etc: a Review of General Semantics*, and in the NeoPoiesis anthology *Candy*. *Wisdom & Dust* is his first poetry collection.

NeoPoiesis
a new way of making

in ancient Greece, poiesis referred to the process of making
creation – production – organization – formation – causation
a process that can be physical and spiritual
biological and intellectual
artistic and technological
material and teleological
efficient and formal
a means of modifying the environment
and a method of organizing the self
the making of art and music and poetry
the fashioning of memory and history and philosophy
the construction of perception and expression and reality

NeoPoiesis Press
reflecting the creative drive and spirit
of the new electronic media environment

Breinigsville, PA USA
12 October 2010
247238BV00001B/11/P